Whitmore Hills

P.S. Winn

This book is a work of fiction, names, places, characters and happenings are a work of the author's imagination.
Any resemblance to people, places or actual happenings is purely coincidental.

Chapter 1

As she walked back from the set of metal mailboxes, Natalie Treston slowly thumbed through her mail. As she expected, most were bills. They'd been piling up since she'd lost her job at Portsmouth Medical Center. When a new administrator had taken over and reorganized the workings of the hospital. That was when a lot of people had been handed their walking papers, including Natalie. She supposed she should be grateful for the severance pay she'd earned after five years at the place and had been given along with the termination papers. At least her six year old car was paid for.

Still, Natalie had to downsize and become more frugal in her spending habits, not that she'd ever been extravagant when it came to spending money. She hardly ever went out and couldn't remember the last time she'd had anyone come to her house. She'd lived in a two bedroom apartment, but had moved to a studio closer to the downtown area of

Portsmouth. For Natalie, things weren't looking too good. If you listened to the news, which she seldom cared to do, unemployment was down, especially in the medical industry. So, why was she still without a job after a year of hunting? Natalie sighed and then stopped walking as she saw the return address on one of the letters she held. Seeing the Whitmore Hills logo in the top left corner, Natalie felt her heart clench, before shaking her head. With her luck lately, the letter was probably a form letter like the hundreds of others she'd received in the past year. The standard, thanks for applying, but you didn't meet our criteria for the position.

Brushing back her shoulder length dark blonde hair, Natalie began walking again and stepped into her apartment. Going to the small table in the area that could almost pass for a kitchen, Natalie sat down.
Turning the letter over and over in her hands, Natalie didn't open it right away. Instead, she thought about Whitmore Hills. The place was a private hospital that specialized in psychiatric care. Usually the

patients at Whitmore Hills had come from other hospitals that had given up on them. When Natalie had still been working at Portsmouth Medical, she'd heard others talking about Whitmore Hills. The pay was good, in fact it was at least double, maybe triple the salary any of the nurses at Portsmouth made. Add to that, employees lived in paid housing behind the center, some just called The Hills.

Despite the great pay and the included housing, no one Natalie knew wanted to work at the place. Natalie, who wasn't close to any of her co-workers, never fully understood their hesitation. She'd listened to the rumors about patients at The Hills being unstable and some even dangerous. Natalie didn't buy into the stories. Any organization that kept its' doors closed to the outside world was subject to speculations that were, more often than not, pessimistic.

Natalie slowly slipped a finger under the white flap of the envelope and slid it under. Opening the letter, it wasn't until the third time she'd read the contents that Natalie finally felt herself breathe normally.

She'd gotten the job.

Swallowing the lump in her throat, Natalie felt like crying with relief. Staring at the letter, she noticed the date for her to come in and talk to a Doctor named Jonas Sullivan was set for the next day. Now, she felt her nerves tense with anxiety. After a year of trying she'd finally been offered a job and it was at a place no one else wanted to work. Shaking the thought from her head, Natalie stood from the table and walked the few feet to an armoire where she hung her clothes. The studio apartment didn't have a closet like a bedroom would, in fact her bed was a futon that sat in the middle of the living area. The only other room in the studio apartment was a bathroom, barely big enough for the five feet two woman to fit in. It was cheap though and until she actually began working at her new job that was all Natalie could afford.

Searching through her clothes, Natalie wondered what the housing at Whitmore Hills would be like. One thing for sure, it had to be an improvement over her situation right now and if what she'd heard about the hospital was right, completely paid for. The brown eyes lit up at that thought. She couldn't wait to get out of this studio apartment and get on with her life. Natalie felt like Whitmore Hills was going to be the answer to her prayers.

*   *   *

Natalie was up early the next morning, despite tossing and turning all night worrying about today's appointment. Skipping breakfast, she mixed up her coffee with a cup of hot chocolate and put it in her large mug. Before poverty struck, she was always grabbing coffee at one of the drive-thru coffee houses that seem to be on every corner. She'd found ways to make her own now and if anyone asked, which no one did, she would have told them her homemade concoctions were better.

Taking her cup and grabbing a light coat, Natalie got in her car. Starting it, she looked in the rear view mirror at her reflection. She never thought she was pretty, maybe cute would be close. She always felt her light brown eyes were too wide for her small face. Her blonde hair was dark enough it was almost brown. Today she had pulled it back into an efficient pony tail for her interview. Actually it was an orientation, since the letter stated she had the job.

Taking a deep breath, Natalie put the car in gear and drove the few miles to Whitmore Hills. The place sat on the outskirts of Portsmouth on five acres of land surrounded by a ten foot chain length fence.

As she pulled into the parking lot, Natalie glanced at her watch and saw she was a half an hour early. She took a moment to glance around. The hospital itself looked old. Natalie heard that it had been a bed and breakfast years ago. It had only been restructured to a hospital five years back. Staring at the off white building in need of a paint job. Natalie hoped the inside looked more modern. She could just see the edge of the apartment complex behind the main building and felt better seeing at least the building back there was better kept. Behind those buildings, Natalie could see the woods and the top of Thompson's Peak looming up above the pine trees. When her parents had still been alive, Peggy and Mitch Treston had enjoyed camping in the Holden National forest, although the camping sites were on the far side from where Natalie sat now. Natalie shook her head, the last thing she needed to do was to bring up memories of her parents. Natalie had been twenty eight when her parents, along with her grandparents on her mother's side had all been killed in a car crash.

Natalie's father's parents had died when Natalie was in grade school. Not long before her parent's died, Natalie had taken a break from three years of nursing and gone back to college to study psychiatry. Taking time away from college after the accident, Natalie had never gone back. Instead she got the job at Portsmouth Hospital and was happy there until a year ago.

Taking one final look at her reflection in the mirror, Natalie got out of the car and walked to the front of Whitmore Hills. The double front doors had no windows and looking to either side, Natalie saw heavy drapes kept

11

any eavesdroppers from looking in. Grasping the handle, surprised the door wasn't locked, Natalie turned the knob and stepped inside. She was immediately greeted by a man standing to the side of the doorway, arms folded over his massive chest. His brown eyes narrowed as he stared at Natalie. His voice, when he spoke was somber. "Can I help you?"

Looking at the man in his dark blue uniform, Natalie's first impression was the guy had to be security. Glancing at his hip where a gun was holstered only reassured her guess. As she answered, Natalie wished her own voice sounded more confidant. "I'm Natalie Treston, I have an appointment scheduled with Doctor Sullivan this morning."

Nodding, the man pointed at a desk about fifteen feet away from where they stood and then hollered over at the man sitting there. "Hey Arthur, is Doc Sullivan expecting someone today?"

The movie star handsome man behind the desk smiled, his blue eyes lighting up. "Yep, looks like we finally might have a replacement for Shelley."

He turned to Natalie. "I'm Arthur, why don't you have a seat over here and I'll let Doctor Sullivan know you're here." Arthur glanced at his watch. "He'll be impressed that you're early."

Nodding, Natalie walked over to the desk and took the seat across from Arthur while he picked up the phone off the desk. She heard him say, your appointment's here, and not much else before he hung up the phone and then, reaching across the desk, held out a hand for her to shake. "Welcome to Whitmore Hills. I'm Arthur Gould, receptionist slash nurse. The big gorilla over by the door is Rex Corgin, don't worry about him, his bark is worse than his bite. He's one of two security guards here at the hospital. You'll meet Vann Shields soon. You can't miss that gleaming bald head of his. According to my papers, you're Natalie Treston, at least you better be or the doc is gonna shoot me."

Natalie smiled, liking Arthur right away. "I'm Natalie, nice to meet you, and yes I'm here for the job."

Arthur smiled. "Great, we've been shorthanded for a couple of weeks. We had a nurse leave unexpectedly. I'm sure you'll like it here."

If Arthur had more to say he didn't finish as a door opened in the hall behind him and a tall thin man in a white coat stepped over to them. He ignored Arthur and Rex and focused his attention on Natalie.
Taking her hand, he smiled and Natalie noticed his eyes were dark gray. She couldn't remember seeing eyes that color before. "Miss Treston, how good of you to show up early. I like punctuality, a good trait in a person. Would you care to come into my office and we can get you ready for your new job."

Nodding, Natalie stood. "Thank you, I'm ready to start a new job too."

Giving Arthur a smile, Natalie then stood and followed Doctor Sullivan back down the hall and to an open door. He stood back to let her enter first. "Just take a chair in front of the desk there. I have all your paperwork in order."

Jonas Sullivan took the seat opposite the desk from Natalie. She noticed the only thing on the desk besides a Manila folder was a kinetic balancing pendulum. She'd seen a few of them, but this one was a bit different than the usual ones. It moved back and forth continuously as Jonas picked up the folder. Jonas looked at Natalie. "I have a standard application form here for you to sign. You are aware that all employees here at Whitmore Hills live on site."

Even though the Doctors words were more a statement than a question, Natalie nodded. "I did know that and would be happy with that arrangement."

The doctor nodded, his gray eyes studying Natalie. "We also ask that you sign an agreement that you will stay employed at least one year. After that we will negotiate a new contract." Jonas slid two pieces of paper and a pen to Natalie.

"If you would just look those over and then sign them, we can have a look at your apartment and then I can introduce you to the others working here. Today is Thursday, could you be moved in over the weekend and start Monday? We've been a bit shorthanded lately."

Picking up the papers, Natalie read through them. Mostly they were like a rental agreement. Stating she would stay at not only the hospital but in her apartment for a year. There was also a non-disclosure statement saying she wouldn't talk about anything she saw at the hospital.

Seeing the frown on her face, the doctor leaned forward. "If you know anything about the medical industry, you must know that much of what we do is kept secret until it can be patented. Many companies would love a chance to steal the work we do here. That form is the little protection we have from that happening. Because we work with mentally ill patients, a lot of what we are doing right now is groundbreaking and will benefit many."

As Natalie nodded and signed the papers, Jonas leaned back and smiled. "Your resume included the fact that you had some schooling in psychiatry, is that right?"

With a shrug, Natalie nodded. "I had two years of schooling. An unfortunate accident caused me to leave school and return to nursing. I have always been fascinated by psychiatry though."

Jonas nodded. "That was one of the reason your application was accepted. We only house a few patients here at Whitmore. I like the personal contact much better than what you find at larger facilities. In fact, at the moment we have only five patients to care for. Besides you, there are three other nurses. Each of you work forty two hours a week. You will be given two days off a week but will also be on call in case of emergencies. If you are called in, of course, you will be well paid for that extra time." Jonas slid the papers Natalie had signed into a folder and then slipped the folder into his desk drawer before standing. "I think that takes care of the paperwork. Oh, one more thing, under emergency contacts on your application, you left the space blank. Isn't there anyone you'd like to put down?"

A small sigh escaped Natalie before she shook her head. "No, I don't have any family." Natalie was thinking that her friend list was just about as long, when the doctor spoke.

"I hope you will count your new co-workers as not only friends, but as family too. It's hard to not have family around. Why don't we go and have a look at your apartment."

Glad the doctor hadn't asked more questions, Natalie followed him out the door and down the hallway. Stepping out the back door of the facility, she looked up and smiled. A bright sun lit up the day, with a few cumulous clouds dotting the sky. The month into spring day was going to be a glorious one. Although they'd had a mild winter, it was still nice to know spring was here. It had always been Natalie's favorite time of year. She loved the green colors of spring and the sounds of singing birds. Even now, as the two walked to the apartment complex, Natalie could hear the chirping of birds not far in the distance. She was thankful for the sound and took it as a sign that she was making the right decision coming to the hospital.

When they made their way to her apartment and Jonas unlocked the door to let her in, Natalie was certain this was the right move for her. The apartment, although just a one bedroom was at least three times larger than her studio apartment. The walls were an off white color and the carpeting a beige and tan mix that Natalie thought would be perfect to keep clean. The apartment was furnished, right down to dishes in the bright peach colored kitchen cupboards. Natalie turned to Doctor Sullivan. "This is great."

The doctor smiled. "You haven't seen the bedroom or the bathroom yet. They are just down this hallway."

Natalie followed Jonas first to the bathroom where she was delighted to see a large garden tub with a shower. Stepping in the bedroom she found a queen size bed. That piece of furniture was the only thing in the apartment she saw that she could tell needed attention. Although the bed and matching dresser were in great shape, the bed needed bedding.

Jonas pointed at the bare mattress. "We feel it is better for tenants to bring their own bedding. I hope this is satisfactory and you can find a way to be moved in by the end of the weekend."

Thinking of her small, almost empty apartment, Natalie smiled. "I don't see a problem with that."

Handing her the key, Doctor Sullivan smiled. "Great, now then, we can have a tour of the hospital. I think it would be better to introduce you to the patients once you have actually started working here. Some of the patients have a bit of a problem with change and introducing you today and then not having you return until Monday might disrupt their lives."

When the two stepped out of the apartment, Natalie used her new key to lock up and then followed the doctor back into the

hospital. He turned to her as soon as they entered. "You've already seen the entrance and my office, the other doctor here is Doctor Fredrick Harrell, his office is next to mine. He isn't here today, but will be back by Monday when you start work."
Jonas pointed to the opposite side of the building from where they were standing. "If you will follow me, I'll show you around the main floor and then we can go upstairs. The facility has a basement also, but it is mostly for storage and janitor supplies."

Natalie was taken first to the cafeteria and shown around and then to a type of recreation room where the doctor said patients could spend free time if they earned it and where celebrations and meetings were held. When they finished the downstairs tour, Natalie followed the doctor up a flight of stairs. As they walked, the doctor turned to Natalie. "You will find a matching set of stairs at the other end of the building and also an elevator. We don't use it often, but sometimes it is easier when moving large items or hurt patients. At this time, all our patients are mobile, so you won't have to concern yourself with that."

When the two stood in the upstairs hallway, Natalie frowned at the sets of closed doors, four on each side of the hall. Seeing the look, Doctor Sullivan gave her a small smile. "We keep the patients room locked for their own safety. We've had a few try to run away and found them lost in the woods. It's better for all if the doors are locked. On Monday, when you meet the patients, you will be given a key."

As the doctor was speaking the door to one of the rooms opened and a woman who looked about ten years older than Natalie's thirty two stepped out. Closing the door behind her, Natalie could hear the sound of the lock engaging. The doctor pointed at the woman. "Rita, I'm glad we caught you. I'd like you to meet Natalie, she will be joining you on Monday. I finally found a replacement for our missing nurse."

Smiling broadly, her dark eyes lighting up with the motion, Rita took Natalie's hand and shook it. "Glad to have you. I don't know if Doctor Sullivan told you, but we've been shorthanded lately. We'll all be glad to get back to normal. Have you worked at a hospital before?"

Natalie nodded. "I've been a nurse for eight years off and on. I took a couple years off in between to go to school."

The head of dark curls bobbed. "That's great, when do you start?"

It was the doctor who answered. "Natalie is going to use the weekend to get moved and then start work Monday. In fact, she has the apartment next to yours."

Rita nodded at the doctor, but turned to Natalie smiling. "If you need any help, just let me know and when you get moved in, come on over to my place and we can get to know each other."

Surprised at the warm reception, Natalie smiled. "That would be great, thanks." In all the time Natalie had worked for Portsmouth hospital she couldn't remember any one welcoming her or inviting her to their place. This new job was going to be amazing.

Rita was smiling at Natalie. "I better get back to work, I'll see you this weekend and remember I'll be right next door to help. I expect you to call on me."

Natalie nodded. "I'll do that, thanks for the offer and it was really nice to meet you."

The brown eyes lit up. "The pleasure was mine."

As Rita walked down to the next door in the hall and unlocked it and stepped inside, Doctor Sullivan turned to face Natalie. "On Monday we'll get you into the rooms and let you meet the patients. Like I said before at the time we only have five patients, so your work load shouldn't be too bad. Even if we fill the other three rooms, I'm sure at the hospital you worked at you had a lot more people to care for."

Natalie nodded. "We did have quite a few patients. I like this better and think it is great for much better personal care."

The doctor nodded. "We all feel the same way. Now, let's go back downstairs. I'm sure you'd like to go and get busy on your moving. If you need help, either I or any of the others here are always good to help, all you have to do is ask."

Natalie smiled. "That's so good of you. I don't have a whole lot to move and since the apartment is furnished, things should go smoothly. If I do need help, I'll be sure to give out a holler."

The strange thing to Natalie was that she felt that if she did ask for help she would gladly be given it. Since the death of her parents, she'd never felt that way. At Portsmouth Hospital her co-workers were so busy with their own lives, they didn't pay the quiet Natalie much attention. Since she wasn't much for going out and partying, after she'd declined the offers a couple times, she wasn't asked again. Natalie found she liked it that way and was happy just spending time at home, mostly reading psychology and medical books.

The two had reached the front desk where Arthur was sitting. He smiled at Natalie. "I hope you approve of our place and will be joining us."

Smiling back, Natalie nodded. "I'll be bringing my first load in the morning. In fact I'm heading home now to start loading my things."

Natalie turned to Doctor Sullivan. "That is if you're done with my orientation."

The doctor nodded and held out his hand. As Natalie shook it, he smiled. "Welcome to Whitmore Hills."

Chapter 2

Leaving the hospital and driving home, Natalie couldn't believe how well all had went at Whitmore Hills. She'd been excited to just get a job. But, add in how friendly everyone had been and a new apartment to the deal and she felt like someone had just handed her a golden ticket.

When she stepped into her tiny apartment, her feeling of being the luckiest person in the world only intensified. Before sorting through her things, Natalie drove to the liquor store to see if they had any empty boxes she could have. Her good luck held up and she loaded her trunk and backseat with boxes.
Stopping for a sandwich at a neighborhood deli, Natalie got her make shift meal to go and then headed home to get busy.

Instead of sitting down to eat, Natalie
opened the sandwich on the counter and
nibbled away at it as she filled boxes with
the few things she needed from her kitchen.
Her cupboards were almost empty and the
food from her fridge went in the garbage.
She lugged several bags to the dumpster that
belonged to the complex before she packed
up her few belongings in her living room
that was also used as a bedroom.

It didn't take her long to pack her meager
belongings into boxes. Natalie had mixed
feelings about that. She was able to be able
to move easily and quickly, but depressed
that her life had been reduced to the few
boxes that were stacked next to the futon in
the tiny living room. She also knew in her
much bigger, new apartment, her belongings
would look even smaller.

She sighed, glad that at least she'd never
been a materialistic person. Looking at the
boxes that contained her clothes, Natalie
frowned. Her wardrobe consisted mostly of
the scrubs she used while working at the
hospital. She hadn't asked Doctor Sullivan if

she'd be given a uniform or what the dress code was for her new job.

Frowning, Natalie tried to remember what Rita had been wearing, but no images came to mind. Deciding sometime over the weekend she'd find someone to ask, Natalie was at least able to drop one worry from her mind.

Heading to the kitchen area, Natalie grabbed a pen and paper, then sat at the table and began a list of things to do so she could complete her move. She knew she would lose her deposit that she'd put down on the studio apartment for not giving a month's notice. She didn't care about the money. All she worried about was making sure the place was clean when she left. Natalie knew it would be cleaner than when she'd moved in.

After she finished her to do list, Natalie fixed a late dinner and then watched the news before, worn out from the day, changed into a nightgown and laid down on the futon bed that had come with the apartment.

Closing her eyes, Natalie replayed her day in her head before finally falling asleep, a satisfied smile on her face.

The next day, Natalie got up early and made several trips to her car with boxes. Taking a few minutes between trips to gulp down the coffee she was calling breakfast. By the time the car was loaded, it was almost lunchtime. Natalie took a moment to make the few phone calls she needed to in order to tie up loose ends for her big move. Rather than making lunch when she finished, Natalie grabbed a protein bar and a bottle of water and then headed to Whitmore Hills.

When she pulled in the same parking lot she had the day before, she noticed a small road that led away from the area and over to another lot in front of the apartment complex. Thankful that she'd be doing less carrying of boxes than she had planned on, Natalie drove over.
Heading to her apartment, Natalie unlocked the door and stepped in. Taking a moment, she glanced around the area, her brown eyes

dancing with delight, before she turned away and got to work.

Before she'd been able to get half the boxes moved, a man a foot taller than Natalie, walked up to her. "Hi, you must be Natalie. Rita said you'd be moving in today. Let me help you with those boxes. I should have been out here sooner, but I worked until four this morning and just woke up."

Staring at the man, Natalie shook her head. With the guy's blonde hair, blue eyes and athletic build, he looked like he should be out on a sunny beach somewhere instead of here at the hospital. "I'm glad for the help, but you're probably still tired. I don't have much to do and have all weekend to do that. Why don't you go and get some rest?"

The man shook his head. "My mom raised me right and if she heard I didn't help a lady when she needed it, she'd give me hell for sure. My name's Carl by the way."

As the man stuck out his hand, Natalie shook it, noticing the hand she held for just a moment was twice as big as her own.

"It's nice to meet you Carl. I'd hate to be the cause of your mom being mad at you. Guess I'll have to take you up on that offer."

Carl winked a blue eye at Natalie. "Good thinking, my mom's sixty three, but she can hold her own in an argument. Now, let's get this stuff moved."

Between the two of them, it didn't take long to empty Natalie's car and stack the boxes in her new apartment. Looking at the small stack, Carl frowned. "Are you going to be making many more trips?"

Natalie shrugged. "I have one more trip to make. I'm waiting until tomorrow to do that. I want to take tonight to clean my old place. Hopefully by tomorrow night I'll be finished and staying here for good."

Carl nodded. "Sounds like a plan. I usually work the night shift, but Rusty will be around tomorrow, he's got the next couple of days off."
Seeing the curious look on Natalie's face, Carl grinned. "Rusty's the other nurse. You can't miss him, he fits his name. The mop of

hair he has really is the color of rust. When I see him, I'll tell him to keep an out for you."

Natalie stared in wonder at Carl. "Thanks, I can't believe everyone has been so nice, but none of you need to go out of your way for me."

Carl laughed. "Well, we all not only work together, but all of us live here in the apartments too. If we didn't get along and help each other, none of us would keep our jobs for long."

Natalie frowned. "Is that what happened to the nurse I'm replacing?"

Carl shrugged. "To tell you the truth, none of us knows what happened. Shelley just didn't show up for work one day. She wasn't at her apartment, but her car was still here. No one's heard from her that I know of. She had family in Florida and I think that's where she was headed. Shelley wasn't really cut out to be a nurse. I hope she's happy back with her family. I know she missed them a lot and was upset she couldn't take time off to go visit them whenever she wanted to."

Natalie nodded, but still thought it strange that the woman would have just left like that. Then she smiled, thinking she was doing almost the same thing, except she didn't have a family she was running to. "I'm sure she's better off with her family then. Thanks again for helping me, I'd offer you a drink or something, but right now my fridge is empty."

Carl laughed. "No problem, I should head back to my place and grab a shower anyway. I'll make sure and tell Rusty to watch for you tomorrow. It was nice meeting you, I hope you'll really like it here."

Natalie smiled. "So far, it's been amazing and everyone has been so nice."

After Carl walked away, Natalie went into her apartment and unloaded a couple of boxes before deciding she better head back for her last night at her old place.

After she got there, Natalie spent the rest of the evening scrubbing the apartment and by the time she was done and had taken a quick shower, she was more than ready for a good night's sleep.

The next day when she pulled in with the last of her belongings in her car, a man, she could easily tell had to be Rusty, was standing outside and waved at her when she pulled in. As he stepped over to her car and then walked over to her, he smiled.
"The famous Natalie. Wow, Carl wasn't lying when he said you were cute as a bug. I'm Rusty, Carl probably didn't tell you how cute I am. Glad to meet you."

Laughing, Natalie took the offered hand. To her, Rusty looked like the typical boy next door. That is if you lived on a farm. For some reason, she could picture Rusty riding a farm tractor and throwing bales of hay. He was about the same height as Carl, but his shoulders were twice as broad.
"Carl didn't say anything about your looks, except I should look for your rust colored hair."

Natalie looked up at the hair, which hung almost to the man's shoulders. "I like the color though."

As Rusty smiled, Natalie could see the humor in the light brown eyes. "I'm glad you do. I like it myself. So, are you ready to put me to work?"

Natalie nodded. "Sure, just let me unlock my apartment."

Running over to unlock the door and then hurrying back out to the car, Natalie stared wide eyed at Rusty, already holding one box under each arm. He smiled. "This shouldn't take long, I like a lady who travels light."

Natalie laughed. "It does make moving a whole lot easier."

After they moved Natalie's boxes, Rusty pointed at the stacks they'd made. "Do you need help unloading those?"

Natalie shook her head. "I can do that. I need to try and decide where everything goes anyway."

The eyes sparkled as Rusty laughed. "My stuff all seem to just end up in a pile in the corner. I hate to move boxes and run, but I promised Doc Harrell, I'd work on his car today. I'll probably see you tomorrow. I have it off too. Rita gets off this afternoon at four. I know she'll be by to check on you."

Natalie smiled. "I'll keep an eye out for her. Thanks a lot for your help."

Rusty shrugged. "I really didn't do much, but I was glad to help."

After Rusty left, Natalie decided to tackle the unloading of the boxes. She'd almost finished when she heard a knock on the door. As she went over and answered the door, she smiled at Rita standing there. "Hi Rita, nice of you to come by. Did you just get off work?"

Rita nodded as Natalie opened the door wider to let her in. She smoothed down her dark blue scrubs. "Can't you tell? Although half the time when I'm not working, I wear the same outfit."

Smiling at that, Natalie nodded. "I'm the same way. I was going to ask you about that. Can we wear our own scrubs or does the hospital have some we have to wear?"

As the two moved to the couch and sat down, Rita shrugged. "We wear our own. In fact, half the time Rusty and Carl wear jeans. The only people that have uniforms are the security guards. Have you met them?"

Natalie frowned. "I met Rex when I came here to meet Doctor Sullivan. Oh, I met Arthur at the front desk too."

Rita smiled. "Actually Arthur is a security guard, a receptionist and a nurse. For all I know he has other talents too. He fills in when anyone gets sick. We have one other guard. Vann Shields, he usually works the overnight shift. So, I guess you've almost met everyone here. Well, except for Doctor Harrell. He usually spends time cooped up in his office or down in the basement. He has all kinds of experiments going on in his lab down there."

Natalie smiled. "Don't forget the patients. I haven't met any of them yet."

Rita laughed. "How could I forget? Without them, none of us would be here. Would you like to hear about them?"
As Natalie nodded, Rita frowned. "Let's go to my place and have a drink. I bet you don't have any food or drinks in here since you've been busy moving."

Realizing Rita was right, Natalie shrugged. "Good thing I have another free day before I start work. I'll go shopping tomorrow."

Rita stood. "Great, and plan on having dinner at my place tonight too."
Natalie started to shake her head, but Rita smiled. "Don't worry, you can pay me back with dinner and drinks after you get settled."

As she nodded, Natalie grinned. "It's a deal, besides, I can't wait to hear about the patients."

Natalie followed Rita to her apartment next door which was similar to her own, although Rita had decorated her place in a southwest style that Natalie thought felt homey and inviting.

Going to her freezer, Rita pulled out a frozen dinner. "I hope you like lasagna. It takes an hour to make. That will give us plenty of time to talk."
As she put the dinner in the oven, Rita looked at Natalie, still standing. "Take a seat at the table. Would you drink a glass of wine? That's what I'm having, but I have a lot of other drinks or I could put on a pot of coffee."

As she sat down, Natalie smiled. "I'd really love a glass of wine."
Natalie didn't drink often, mostly because she didn't like to drink alone and that seemed to be how she spent most of her time. Especially after her parents had died. Natalie sighed as she realized that had been four years ago. She looked up as Rita handed her a glass.

"Here you go. Are you okay, you look a little tired?"

Glad Rita had mistook her depression for tiredness, Natalie nodded. "I'm fine, I guess I'm still trying to adjust. You know, a new job, a new apartment and meeting everyone all is a matter of a couple of days."

As Rita took a seat, she nodded and smiled. "In no time, you'll feel like you've been here forever. I know I feel that way."

A frown creased Natalie's forehead. "How long have you been here?"

A sigh escaped Rita's lips. "I've been a nurse at The Hills almost four years now. I hope I'll only be here one more. The pay here is damn good and hopefully in a year I'll have enough saved up to retire."

Staring at Rita, Natalie shook her head. "You're pretty young to think about retiring."

Rita laughed. "I'm forty three, but I also have an inheritance from my grandparents to help. What I'd like to do more than anything else is buy me a motorhome and travel across the country."

As she looked at Rita, a smile broke out on Natalie's face. "That would be fun. Do you have family that would travel with you?"

Rita shook her head. "Not really. My parents have a condo in Arizona, but I don't have any other family. I might have a cousin or two floating around somewhere, but none I stay in touch with. No one working here is married, has kids or a family close by. I think Doctor Sullivan hires single people on purpose. No close ties to interfere with our work."

The brown eyes staring at Rita turned down in a frown. "What about the doctors that work here?"

Rita laughed. "If either of them are married, I've never heard about it. I think both Doctor Sullivan and Doctor Harrell are married to their jobs. When they aren't working with the patients, they're down in that lab of theirs. No one knows what goes on in that place."

The brown eyes widened. "I thought they just had storage down in the basement."

Taking a drink of her wine, Rita nodded. "Oh, there's a lot of stuff down there, but those two have a lab also. They do a lot of experimenting on new medications to help the patients."

Lifting her own glass, Natalie smiled and then took a drink before asking what she felt was the most important question. "What are the patients like?"

Shrugging, Rita smiled. "We only have five and they're all a bit different. I don't want to share too much about my feelings about each of them. I want you to form your own opinions, but I can tell you what they look like and why they're getting treatment here. First you should know Whitmore Hills is known for taking patients other hospitals have given up on. I don't think any of the five are dangerous. Although we've had a bad episode here and there."
Rita put a finger to her lip and tapped it, thinking. "Let's start with the women. We have two in our small group, Megan Swanson and Abby Benson. I guess Abby's about your age, what are you almost thirty?"

Nodding, Natalie smiled. "I'm thirty two."

Rita laughed. "Actually you look younger, but I was guessing high because I figured you had a lot of experience or you wouldn't have gotten hired."

Rita shrugged. "Not that age and experience always go hand in hand. Anyway, Abby is thirty. Poor thing, she's even shorter than me." Rita shook her head. "She's such a tiny thing with dark hair and eyes."

Running a hand through her own dark hair, Rita smiled. "Even darker than mine. Abby has major depressive disorder. She's tried to commit suicide on a couple of occasions."

Looking at the sorrow that filled Natalie's face, Rita nodded. "I think all five of our patients suffer from one form of depression or another. The other woman, Megan is younger, just twenty three. She has what's called a dissociative identity disorder. I haven't seen her, let's say, wild side. According to her records, her alter ego calls herself Trixie."

Rita smiled. "Great name right? Anyway, it seems Trixie liked to spend her time in bars and with any man who'd buy her a drink. That girl's damn lucky she hasn't tested positive for any diseases."

Natalie shook her head, her dark blonde hair, now loose, swinging side to side with the motion. "That's too bad. I've read about the problem, but never actually seen it. In fact, most of my experience with psychiatric patients was at college, a long time ago."

Rita laughed. "You'll learn quickly. There's not much difference in being a nurse here or any other hospital. You take care of your patients the best you can and hope you make a difference."

Grabbing her glass, Rita took another drink before continuing. "Now, to the male side of things. We have Steve Lincoln, Ted Clark and Tony Conroy. Steve and Ted are both in their forties and Tony is your age. Steve is a manic depressive with bi-polar. His moods are up and down like a yo-yo. Steve is a handsome guy with blonde hair and blue eyes that light up when he's happy and appear two shades darker when he's in his down moods. Ted is a roly-poly guy."

Seeing Natalie frown, Rita laughed. "He's a bit on the heavy side and suffers from non-Alzheimer's dementia. Of all the patients, I'd say Ted is the optimist. He's almost always in a good mood. His memory is full of big gaping holes, but Ted fills them with some whopping stories. If he tells you any story, it's best to dismiss it as made up." Rita sighed. "That just leaves Tony." Grabbing her glass, Rita tipped it and finished what was left. She wiggled her empty glass. "I need a refill, how about you?"

Natalie shook her head. "I better not or I'll end up falling asleep. I usually only have one or two when I drink and that's not often."

Rita nodded. "Me either, but all this talking is making me thirsty."
As she got up and refilled her wine, Rita stopped to check on their dinner before joining Natalie back at the table.
"Let's see, I think we're down to Tony. Like I said, he's your age. Tony has delusions. He also suffers from paranoia and maybe a bit

of bi-polar. He also has the most beautiful eyes I've ever seen. They're not just an incredible shade of green, but they have these golden specks in them. When he's in a good mood, they seem to dance. He also has a head of thick chocolate brown hair.

"I'm sure a lot of women followed that guy around."

Now, Rita stared at Natalie and shook her head. "Despite his handsome good looks and quiet manner, Tony is the one patient I think you need to be on your guard with. When he came to Whitmore Hills, he arrived in the back of a police car. Tony was found in an alley in Portsmouth covered in blood. His story is that he was attacked by a creature from another world. Something about being lost in that place and barely escaping with his life. The blood on Tony was tested and luckily it wasn't human. I don't know if they ever decided exactly where the blood came from or not. The fact that it wasn't human blood, landed Tony here at The Hills instead of spending a lifetime behind bars somewhere."

Staring at Natalie, Rita hoped she hadn't frightened her. She just wanted Natalie to be prepared. As the buzzer of the oven went off, Rita stood and stared down at Natalie. "Tony has always been gentle as a mouse while he's been here, but I thought you'd be better off knowing about his past."

Natalie nodded. "I'm glad you told me."

Rita shrugged. "It's all there in his files, but I thought it would be better if you heard it from me than to find it as a surprise while reading it in his record. We have access to the computers at work. I don't know if you had time to notice or not, but the apartment complex doesn't have internet service. The doctors have rules about us being on-line except at work."

Natalie frowned. "I wondered about that, isn't it a bit strange. Why would they stop us from going on-line on our own time?"

Rita shrugged. "I guess it's a security thing. That way we can't divulge any secrets the doctors are working on. They tell me the pharmaceutical industry is pretty cut throat.

Both of the doctors have patented quite a few medications and are always working on new drugs and treatments."

Rita sighed. "We are all used to it. Now, I think I better get our food before it burns. You'd never accept another invite for dinner from me again."

As the two ate their meal, they didn't mention the patients again. Instead they spent the time talking mostly about the places Rita would like to visit and setting a more up-beat mood.

By the time Natalie left to go back to her apartment, she felt like she'd known Rita for years and not just the few hours they'd actually spent in each other's company.

As Natalie got ready for bed and then crawled wearily under the covers, her exhaustion didn't prevent the images that floated in her mind. Pictures of a man with green eyes being viciously attacked by a strange beast.

The next morning. Natalie woke up, disoriented for a moment. Looking around the room, her confusion left and she smiled, happy for a new beginning.

Getting out of bed, she remembered she didn't have any coffee or food in her place. Dressing quickly, Natalie grabbed her car keys and headed to town. Stopping for a quick breakfast at a neighborhood café, Natalie then headed to the grocery store for much needed supplies.

She was able to put all her groceries away and finishing organizing her new apartment before she answered a knock on her door.

When she opened the door, she smiled, seeing Rita and Carl standing there, each carrying in a pizza box in their hands. Inviting them in, Natalie spent the last evening before beginning her new job in the company of people she had already began to think of as her friends.

Chapter 3

The sound of her alarm clock woke Natalie
from a sound sleep. Reaching over, she hit
the switch to silence the noise and then
stretched out. She smiled, glad to be waking
up in a real bed instead of the narrow futon
she had been using.

Getting up, Natalie made coffee and decided
to just grab toast for breakfast. Her stomach
was already in knots worried about her first
day at her new job.

Natalie was finished and dressed for work
early enough that she walked around the
outside of the apartment complex, admiring
the tall pine trees and studying the area
before she walked the short distance to the
hospital. Stepping in the back door, she
walked down the hall and out to the front
desk, where Arthur was sitting.

He turned as Natalie approached. "Well, there's a beautiful sight to begin my day. Are you ready for your first shift?"

Taking in a deep breath, Natalie nodded. "I think I am. I wasn't sure where to go."

Standing, Arthur smiled. "Doctor Sullivan will take care of everything. C'mon, we'll let him know you're ready."

Natalie followed Arthur to Doctor Sullivan's door. As soon as Arthur knocked on the door, the two could hear the sound of the doctor's voice answering. "C'mon in, the door's open."

Arthur pushed open the door and stuck his head in. "Natalie's here for her first day."

Doctor Sullivan stood smiling.
"Thank you Arthur."
He turned to Natalie, as Arthur left and headed back to his desk. "Good morning Natalie. I hope you were able to get all moved in."

Natalie nodded. "Everything went smoothly. I got a lot of help from the others. Everyone has been so friendly."

The doctor nodded. "That's good to hear. I pride myself on trying to hire the best help. I bet you're anxious to begin work. Let's head upstairs. Rita will be working with you for your first couple of shifts and then if you feel good about it, you can be on your own. I'm afraid we didn't talk about shift preferences and right now the available one is the four to midnight shift. I hope that sounds satisfactory to you."

Natalie nodded. "I'm fine with that. I worked all kinds of shifts at Portsmouth Hospital, so I'm good with any hours."

As the doctor nodded, he led the way and the two went up to the second floor. Doctor Sullivan was pointing at the closed doors. "During your shift you will be required to spend time with each patient. You are responsible for not only their physical but their mental needs as well. Each day, you will be given a set of questions tailored to the individual patients. You will also be responsible to keep a record of their answers on the computer. Doctor Harrell and I use those answers to decide treatments for each patient. Of course, you will also record all the patient's vital signs and it will be your job to clean their rooms. We feel it is best not to employ an outside cleaning service. The guards do any maintenance work that is needed."

Natalie was nodding her understanding and agreement with the doctor's instructions, when she saw a frown cross his face.
"By the way, did you go to town and do shopping yesterday?"

Nodding, Natalie smiled. "I did, unfortunately my fridge and cupboards were bare."

The doctor nodded, already knowing she had been gone. "Of course, that's understandable. I really didn't give you much notice. I should let you know that we ask our employees to limit their trips to town. Usually to once a month. I know that may seem a bit strict and maybe unusual, but we like to keep the employees close by."

The doctor smiled, trying to lessen the harshness of his words. "Just in case an emergency arises. I hope you understand and are agreeable with that."

Natalie couldn't help the slight frown that creased her forehead, but she nodded. "Other than for getting groceries, I think everything I need is right here."

Doctor Sullivan nodded. "That's how we feel and you can also have your meals in the cafeteria. Free of charge of course. Someone is on duty in the kitchen for all meals. Also the kitchen is always open to employees when the cafeteria isn't staffed."
The doctor smiled. "Now that we've taken care of all that, I think we should catch up with Rita. She always begins her day with Megan. When you begin your shifts alone, I'm sure you will have your own schedule and preferences for the order of your day. However you decide is fine as long as each patient is visited."

Natalie followed the doctor to one of the doors. He pulled out a card and handed it to Natalie. "You'll need this to get in the rooms. The doors are to remain locked at all times. Mostly for the patient's own safety." Then he pulled out what looked to Natalie like a cell phone. "This is yours also. You can call any of the nurses or one of the guards with this."

Opening the device, Natalie saw it wasn't quite the same as a cell phone. Instead of a normal keypad, the front only had three colored buttons. The doctor pointed at them. "You use that like a regular cell phone to talk. Making a call is easier though, the yellow button will get you in contact with the nurse who is on call. The blue button will get you a guard and the red one will connect you to either myself or Doctor Harrell. I know you haven't met him yet, but he will be here in an hour or two so the two of you can finally meet. Why don't you go ahead and use your card to open the door."

Natalie nodded and slipped her card into the slot just below the doorknob. As she did, she heard a slight dinging noise and turned the knob and pushed in on the door.

As the two stepped into the room, the first thing Natalie noticed was the room wasn't like an average hospital room. The main item in the room was still a hospital bed, but much nicer than any she'd seen before. The room held a heavy wooden dresser and also a table with two chairs.

On the other side of the bed, she saw a recliner and next to it a door, she knew must lead to a bathroom. Looking around at the paneled walls, Natalie also noticed what she was sure were cameras on the ceiling. She could understand why that was needed, the patients would have to be monitored.

Looking back toward the bed, Natalie smiled at Rita who was standing next to the bed where a young woman was sitting up against several pillows.

Rita smiled. "Hi Natalie, glad you're here." Rita turned to the woman on the bed. "Megan, this is Natalie. She's going to be helping with the nursing here."

Natalie stepped over to the bed. "Hi Megan, it's nice to meet you."

The large brown eyes stared at Natalie, but the woman didn't speak. Instead she pushed herself back against the pillows and then turned to look at Rita, who smiled.
"It's okay Megan, Natalie's a friend. She's here to take care of you. Don't worry you can trust her, you have my word on that."

Doctor Sullivan remained standing by the door as he watched the interaction. Clearing his throat, he looked at Rita. "If you're okay showing Natalie your routine, I'll be going. Lots of work to do, like always. Could you bring Natalie to the cafeteria at lunchtime? I'd like her to meet Doctor Harrell."

Rita nodded. "We'll be fine and I'll bring her down later."

Doctor Sullivan nodded and headed out the room. Natalie noticed Megan's brown eyes had narrowed as they watched the doctor leave.

As soon as he was gone, Megan smiled and nodded. "I'm glad he's gone." She pointed at Natalie, but looked at Rita. "She can stay, if you're sure she's okay."

Laughing, Rita patted Megan's arm. "I wouldn't have said she was if it wasn't true. Now, tell me how you are feeling. Yesterday you said your stomach was hurting."

Megan smiled. "It's okay now, I must have just ate something bad."

Rita nodded. "I'm glad to hear that." She turned to Natalie. "I've already taken Megan's vitals, her blood pressure was slightly elevated, but not enough to worry about it. We see that in her a few times during each month."
Reaching over to the table next to Megan's bed, Rita picked up a clipboard. "Are you ready to answer a few questions?"

The brown eyes frowned. "Don't the doctors ever run out of questions?"

The smile Rita gave her was filled with patience and compassion. "Every question is helpful. Your answers give the doctors the information they need to get you better and then get you on your way out of here. You'd like that wouldn't you?"

Nodding, Megan sighed and ran a hand through her dark hair. "Sometimes I do and other times I feel like it would just be easier to stay here forever instead of returning to the real world. That place isn't always friendly. At least here no one makes fun of me."

Shaking her head, Rita frowned. "Oh c'mon now Megan. Don't you miss being around people? Surely you had friends. In here you only get to talk to us nurses and the doctors."

The shoulders lifted in a shrug. "I guess you're right, I did have a few friends. Okay, let's get to the questions."

Rita took a seat at the table and motioned for Natalie to join her. Looking down at her clipboard, Rita then looked over at Megan. "Are you feeling depressed today?"

The eyebrows drew down as Megan thought about the question. Then she shook her head. "Not really, I didn't sleep well last night. I had a bad dream."

Looking at her list of questions, as she wrote down the answer Megan had given, Rita was glad to see that question three of the short list of five concerned dreams. She nodded. "Do you want to tell us about the dream you had?"

The brown eyes grew wide. "I don't know if I want to talk about it. Maybe I'd be better off to just forget about it."

Looking up at Megan, Rita gave her a slight grin. "And maybe talking about it will chase away your fears. Let's give it a try."

Taking a deep breath, Megan finally nodded. "I was in a place I've never seen before. Mostly I remember it was hot and red. Everything was red. I was alone, but I felt there were others around. Maybe they were hiding. I heard a loud noise and looked up and saw the top of a mountain throwing out fire. I think it was a volcano. I didn't know where to run. When I turned away from that mountain and looked around, every place I looked another mountain was doing the same thing. Then a river of red started to head toward me. Even before it got to me, I could feel the heat. I started to run but another stream blocked my way. I was looking all around when I heard the sound of a bird. It made this loud noise, almost like a scream. Looking up I saw this enormous bird coming toward me, its claws wide open. The thing was big enough it could easily carry me away and I knew that's what it planned on doing."

Megan stopped talking as her breathing quickened. Reaching up, she wiped a hand over her face. "It was awful. I knew that thing was going to kill me and I had nowhere to go. Just as I felt its claws dig into my shoulder, I woke up."
Megan was shaking her head as her hand covered her mouth.

To Natalie, it looked like the woman was about to be sick. Rita saw it too and stood and went over to the bed and slipped an arm around Megan's shoulders. "It's okay Megan, you're okay. Just a dream. You know nothing like that could really happen don't you?"

As Megan nodded, Rita was frowning and thinking that Megan's dream sounded almost like one of Tony Conroy's stories of the other worlds he claimed to have visited. For a moment, she felt there really was some kind of strange connection between the two patients, then she shook the thought from her head and went back to comforting Megan.

After the woman settled down, Rita asked her the last three questions on the list, which thankfully weren't any to cause Megan more distress.
At the bottom of the paper where she'd been recording the answers to the questions, Rita wrote down, sleeping pills, followed by a question mark. She didn't think it was a good idea for Megan to continue having the strange dream or another like it that would upset her.

After making sure Megan was calmed back down, Rita and Natalie left the room and stepped out into the hallway.

Natalie turned to stare at Rita. "Is that normal? That was pretty intense."

Rita shrugged. "It was at that. I'm going to see if one of the doctors will let Megan have a sleeping pill for the next few nights. At least being that upset didn't bring out her alter ego. I was kind of worried it might." Rita checked her watch. "I think we have time to visit with Steve and then we can head to the cafeteria so you can meet Doctor Harrell. I can ask about a sleeping pill for Megan then too. After lunch we can finish up with Ted, Abby and Tony."

Nodding, Natalie took a breath, hoping meeting Steve would be less intense than the visit with Megan had been.

Chapter 4

As Natalie waited for Rita to pull out her key to open Steve's door, she couldn't stop thinking about what had just happened. Natalie didn't care for the way Rita had looked when Megan had talked about her nightmare. She was sure Megan hadn't noticed the way Rita's face had paled for just the briefest of moments.

Rita had finally pulled out her card, but before she got the chance to unlock the door, Natalie put a hand on her shoulder.

"Maybe we should talk about what really happened in Megan's room before we go into Steve's."

As Rita started to shake her head in denial that anything was wrong, she saw the concern on Natalie's face and with a sigh, changed the motion to a nod. "I'm sure it wasn't anything to be concerned about.

Megan's explanation of her nightmare just threw me for a moment. I'm almost certain I've heard that same story before. Although that tale wasn't from a nightmare. I think Megan was describing one of the places Tony Conroy swears he actually traveled to."

Natalie frowned. "Has something like this happened before?"

Rita shook her head. "Not to me and I've never heard anyone else mention it either."

Natalie frowned. "Maybe Tony told Megan about that place."

The head of dark hair shook back and forth as Rita's eyes narrowed. "I don't think so. The patients rarely interact. They only get together for an overnight outing one day a month. That's when they take a trip with Doctor Sullivan and Doctor Harrell. I'm sure the patients don't have much to say to each other when they go either."

Natalie frowned. "What kind of trips are those and where do they go?"

Rita looked at her watch. "They head into the woods. Doctor Sullivan has a cabin there. I think I can explain this better later when we have more time. We need to check on Steve and then get you down to the cafeteria. We can't have you being late for your meeting."

Natalie sighed. "Okay, but I'm gonna hold you to that explanation."

Rita nodded. "I promise, I'll fill you in. In fact, the next trip is only a week away. I should have filled you in on it before. I haven't had to train anyone in a while, sorry if I'm a bit forgetful."
Rita slipped her card into the slot on Steve's door and pushed it open. "For now, we need to focus on our job."

Knowing Rita was right, Natalie nodded and tried to forget about now only this incident, but the story about Tony and the beast Rita had shared the other night. It would seem Tony Conroy's mind took him to some strange places. Natalie also tried not to think about what kind of trips the doctors would be taking the patients on.

As the two stepped in Steve's room, Natalie's thoughts easily transferred to the handsome man standing by his bed.

The blonde haired, blue eyed man was waving frantically. "Hi Rita, did you bring a visitor today?"

Nodding, Rita smiled, glad to find Steve in an elevated mood today. After the episode with Megan, talking to Steve in one of his depressed states wasn't something Rita wanted to do or something she wanted Natalie to see. She placed her clipboard on the table before looking over at her patient. "Hi Steve, looks like you got up on the right side of the bed today. I did bring someone to see you, but Natalie's going to be working here, she's the new nurse."

Smiling and nodding, Steve stepped over and grabbed Natalie's hand. "It's really nice to meet you, I'm Steve."

Looking in the sparkling light blue eyes that seemed to be dancing, Natalie smiled. "It's nice to meet you too, Steve."

Looking over at the two of them Natalie smiled. "Steve, do you want to come sit on the bed and I can have Natalie check and see how you're doing today."

Turning to look at Rita, Steve smiled. "Sure, I can do that. Today, anything you want."

Rita pointed toward the doorway that led to the bathroom. "If you want to head in the bathroom Natalie, I'll show you the closet with the same lock that is on all the room doors. You'll need your key to get in there and I can explain everything to you."

Steve took his place on the bed while the two nurses headed into the bathroom. Natalie used her key card and opened the closet door. Behind her, Rita pointed at the shelves. "You'll find the equipment you need in here to check patients vital signs, also their medications if they take any and a lot of cleaning supplies. I was already done with this part of my duties by the time you came into Megan's room this morning or I would have shown you then."
Rita lifted her hand to touch a printout taped to the inside of the closet down. "This is the

list of Meds. Steve will only takes a blood pressure pill when he is in the mood he is today. He takes an anti-depressant before bed and in the day if needed." Rita laughed. "Definitely none needed today. When you take over the four to midnight shift, you'll always give him one."

Natalie looked at the paper where the instructions were also written. She reached in and took out the bottle of blood pressure pills. "Do you want me to give him one now?"

Rita nodded. "You can if you want. I have a set routine. I usually come in here and clean before I began with the meds and checking the patient's vitals. Since we're both here, you can go ahead and start with Steve and I'll straighten up in here. I shouldn't be long."

As Natalie nodded, she opened the pills and shook one out into her hand before closing the lid and checking the label against the list on the door. Rita smiled, liking that Natalie had done that.

Stepping back out into the room, Natalie smiled at Steve. "I have your medicine, do you need a drink?"

Steve shook his head. "I'm good, I have water over here and a soda."

Stepping to the bed, Natalie handed Steve the pill and watched him take it before she went back to the bathroom and grabbed the blood pressure cuff and thermometer. Returning to Steve's side at the bed, Natalie took his temperature and then his blood pressure, frowning at the high reading.

Natalie stepped out of the bathroom and saw the look. "Steve's pressure goes up when his mood does. You probably found his heart rate high also."
Natalie went to the table where she'd sat down her clipboard. Picking it up, she walked over to stand next to Natalie.
"Under the papers with the questions we need, you can find a bit of information on the patients. Everything is also recorded on the hospital's computers. I'll show you that later. With only five patients it won't take

you long to remember what's normal and what's not for each of them."

Natalie thanked Rita and then smiled at Steve. "Looks like you're doing okay then."

Nodding Steve smiled back. "That's good to hear, but I already knew that. I feel great today."

Rita nodded. "Good, then I guess you won't mind answering a few questions."

Sitting back on his bed, Steve laid back against the headboard and stretching out his legs crossed them at the ankles. "Ready whenever you are."

Rita was laughing as she turned to Natalie. "If you want to lock that equipment back up, I'll let you ask the questions today."

Nodding, Natalie hurried to the bathroom, put everything away, locked the closet door and then came back out into the room where she saw Rita was sitting at the table.
She handed the clipboard to Natalie. "If you have any problems, I'll be right here."

Taking the board, Natalie smiled. "Thanks, that makes me feel better."

As Natalie looked at the questions she saw there was two sets under Steve's name. She could also see the headline above each set stating one group was for during his depressive state and the other for when he was closer to euphoria. Looking at the first question, Natalie then stared at Steve. "Are you an artist Steve?"

Hearty laughter filled the room. "Before I came here, I tried my best to make a living at being one."

Natalie smiled and then asked the question she'd just read. "What would be the most beautiful picture you could think of to paint?"

Staring at Natalie the blue eyes lit up. "Funny you should ask that, I was just thinking earlier if I had my brushes and paints I would be working on a special landscape. I woke up with a picture in my mind of a special place. I don't know if you believe in Heaven, but this image I have is what I feel Heaven must look like. A lot like the Garden of Eden in the bible. You know, plenty of green and a beautiful blue sky, maybe a big lake." Steve smiled. "And of course a beautiful young woman, maybe taking a swim."

Natalie smiled. "That sounds great. I'd love to see your artwork."

With a shrug, Steve sighed. "I don't have any here, but I bet I still have a website if you get near a computer. Just look up Art by Lincoln dot com. Not very original but it works."

Nodding, Natalie grinned. "I'll be sure and do that."

She looked at the list again and then slowly went through the next four questions, before she and Rita finished up with Steve and left the room.

When they stepped out in the hall, Rita smiled at her. "You did great. Steve really seemed comfortable with you."

Natalie laughed. "In the mood he was in, I think Steve would have been comfortable with about anyone, but I found it interesting. It's funny, but you see the patients in here with their problems and forget they had a life before they got put in this place."

Nodding. Rita smiled. "That's easy to forget. Let's go downstairs and I'll show you the computer room before we head to the cafeteria. I think we have time to record this information before you have to meet with the doctors."

After going down the stairs the two went down the hall to the hospital's computer room. As they stepped in, Natalie saw the monitors on the walls that had to be hooked to the cameras that she'd noticed in the patient's rooms. Rita saw her staring up. "We have a set in here and a set in the guard's rooms. The patients are monitored twenty four seven. Usually by the guards. I forget those are even here when I'm recording everything into the computers." Rita looked at Natalie and grinned. "I hope you can type. The doctors like all the vitals from the patients and the answers they give to the questions put in the computer before we get off our shift every day."

Natalie laughed. "I don't care for it, but yeah, I can type."

Rita showed Natalie how to set up a user name and password and then how to find each patients files so they could add information to them. When they finished, Rita smiled. "I usually wait and do all the typing and recording at the end of my shift, but we got finished with Steve early. Plus I usually see three of the patients, then take lunch and check on the last two after that. You can do all that however works best for you, especially since you'll be working the shift you are."
Rita stood. "Are you ready to go meet Doctor Harrell?"

Natalie nodded and Rita frowned. "We actually don't see much of him. Doctor Sullivan is more hands on than Doctor Harrell. I think he likes experimenting in the lab better than interacting with people."

Following Rita from the computer room, Natalie looked around as they headed to the cafeteria. Doctor Sullivan had walked her through the hospital, but it had happened so quickly and she'd been so anxious getting the job she hadn't paid that much attention. The hospital wasn't all that big especially after being at Portsmouth Hospital and Natalie didn't think she'd have any problem finding her way around.

When the two stepped in the cafeteria they saw the two doctors were already seated at a table. Seeing them, Doctor Sullivan stood, followed by the gray haired, heavy set man who'd been sitting with him.

Unlike Doctor Sullivan's dark gray eyes, Doctor Harrell's were almost as dark a blue color as the ones Natalie had just seen in Steve's room were light.

He held out a hand as Natalie and Rita walked up. Taking Natalie's hand, he turned to Rita before talking to Natalie. "It's good to see you Rita." Then he turned back to Natalie. "And you must be the new addition. Glad to have you here with us at Whitmore Hills. I hope you are finding it suitable."

Natalie nodded. "Thank you, I am. It's good to meet you. Everyone here has made me feel so welcome."

The doctor smiled. "I'm glad to hear that. Why don't you two ladies grab something to eat and then we can all sit down together."

Rita led the way to the buffet style counter and the two grabbed their food before coming back to the table. When they sat down, Rita turned to Doctor Sullivan. "Megan is having nightmares. I put it in my report. But I think she may need something to help her sleep tonight."

The gray eyes narrowed, but then the doctor nodded. "I'll make sure to stop by and see her personally before I get off duty tonight. If she still needs something then, I'll administer it myself."

Rita and Natalie spent a few minutes chatting with the doctors, while they ate. Both of the men apologized for having to get back to duties and left half way through the women's meal.

As soon as they left, Rita laughed. "I'm kind of glad they had to go. I never can find much to talk about with either of the doctors. I'd much rather spend my time talking to the patients."

Natalie nodded. "I feel the same, but both of them are much better than the administrator who took over at Portsmouth Hospital. No one could seem to talk to that guy. He was only worried about profits and to hell with patient care. I'm so glad I'm out of that place."

Shaking her head, Rita sighed. "I know all about places like that. One thing you can say is the doctor's here seem to worry about the patients, and I know Doctor Harrell is always trying to come up with new treatments. He's patented quite a few new drugs that have been working well for many psychiatric patients."

Natalie stared at Rita, impressed and delighted to hear that.

Chapter 5

A short time later the two women were back upstairs and standing outside yet another closed door. Rita turned to Natalie before she opened the door. "By now the guards should have gotten everyone's lunch delivered, eaten and the mess cleaned up. They usually serve the patients meals while the nurses on duty are in the cafeteria having their own meal."

Pointing back at the door, Rita smiled. "This is Ted Clark's room. You should know that whatever story Ted is living in on any given day, we just go along with him. I've never seen Ted depressed and most of his stories are fun. As long as he doesn't head down a dark road, no harm to him or to anyone doing the listening."

When Natalie nodded that she understood. Rita opened the door and the two stepped in the room. A broad smile lit the face of the pudgy man sitting on the bed. His cheeks, lifting with the motion, caused his eyes to narrow until they were nothing more than slits. "Well, what do we have here? Not one, but two beautiful women come to visit. That's a sight I don't see every day. Come on in and have a seat. The name's Ted and who would you lovely ladies be?"

Rita laughed. "It's just me, Rita, and I've brought Natalie with me. We're here to see how you are feeling today."

Ted reached over and patted the bed next to him. "Plenty of room. I was just thinking how nice it would be to have some company and like magic, here you are."

Stepping over to the bed, Rita touched Ted's leg. "We'll be glad to visit Ted. Would it be okay if we took a minute to check your temperature and your blood pressure first though?"

Now the brown eyes frowned before Ted shrugged. "I guess you can, but I was thinking we should have ourselves a little party."

Laughing, Rita turned to Natalie, who was smiling at Ted's attitude. "Natalie, would you get everything ready and then do the honors?"
As Natalie nodded and headed for the bathroom, Rita turned back to Ted.
"Actually Ted, Natalie and I are both nurses. We'll be taking care of you."
Compassion filled Rita's eyes, she couldn't imagine how hard it was to not remember not only just a day ago, but most of the life you had led.

It didn't take long for Natalie and Rita to take care of Ted's medical needs and then ask him the few questions that had been designed for him and we are the list.

Both women hated leaving Ted's room when they had finished the visit. He'd been so excited to have them there. His brown eyes had looked so sad when the two had explained they had to leave.

In the hall, Rita smiled at the look on Natalie's face. "Don't worry, he'll be fine. With Ted's imagination, he'll be conjuring up a story to keep him occupied. Time to check on Abby."

As the two moved to the next door, Rita pointed to the clipboard Natalie held. "Abby Benson, despite taking several types of anti-depressants, isn't doing well with treatment. Some days, well most days, we have a hard time getting her to even eat."

Natalie frowned. "I was going to ask about that. If the guards take care of the meals, how do you know if the patients have eaten?"

Rita laughed. "Once again, I'll have to apologize for the lack of information. I'm not very good at training. When the guards clean up after the meals, they record everything in the computer as to what was eaten, that includes snacks and drinks throughout the day. I usually access the patients files before I begin my shift to see how the day before went. The guards are also responsible for keeping a count on any utensils used or other things taken in the patient's rooms. You never know when someone might try to steal a fork or other item to use as a weapon or God forbid to hurt themselves with."

With a sigh, Natalie nodded. She knew first-hand about episodes like that. She supposed most nurses had experience with suicidal patients coming up with strange, inventive ways to hurt themselves or others. Here in the psychiatric hospital, the probability of that happening had to be magnified.
Natalie waited while Rita unlocked the door. As the two stepped in the room, identical frowns lined their faces, seeing an empty room.

Rita pointed at the closed bathroom door. "Abby must be in there."
Stepping to the door, Rita knocked and raised her voice to be heard through the shut door. "Abby, it's Rita, time to get checked." She waited a moment for a response. When she heard none, Rita reached down and turned the knob on the door that had no lock. Pushing the door inward, Rita held her

breath, afraid of what she might find. Stepping in, she saw a shape on the floor of the shower. Abby was curled into a ball in the far corner of the shower. Because of the amount of blood puddled beneath the woman, both Rita and Natalie, standing behind her, knew they were too late to help the woman. Despite knowing that, Rita still knelt down next to the shower and reaching over touched the side of Abby's bent neck. At the absence of a pulse, Rita felt like screaming in agony and sorrow for the loss of a life. Instead, she turned to Natalie. "Call a guard and tell them we need an ambulance, then call and get Doctor Sullivan up here."

Natalie nodded, but still took the time to ask the question she sadly already knew the answer to. "Is she dead?"

Standing, Rita nodded. "She's gone and we need to move out of this bathroom. We don't want to contaminate the area."

By the time Rita pulled the door closed and stepped back from the bathroom, Natalie had already pulled the cell phone from her pocket and pushed first the blue button to reach the guard and then the red one that connected her to Doctor Sullivan.

While the women waited for help to arrive, Natalie turned to Rita shaking her head. "How could Abby have been able to do that? You said the guards kept track of anything deemed to be a weapon."

Rita sighed. "Unfortunately, where there's a will, there's always a way. I'm sure an investigation will be done by not only the doctors here, but also by the police force in Portsmouth. There's no doubt this was a suicide. How or where Abby found a weapon to use will have to be probed. I just wish I would have realized she was that close. She didn't act upset yesterday and I didn't see anything listed on her report this morning."

Rita shook her head. "Not that we can tell what's going on in someone's mind. Unfortunately we work with patients who are extremely depressed."

The two didn't have to wait long before first Rex Corgin, then Doctor Sullivan stepped in the room. While Rex stepped in the bathroom to look at Abby's body, Doctor Sullivan questioned Rita and Natalie. After getting their information, Doctor Sullivan assured them he would take care of matters and asked them to continue their rounds. He also requested nothing be said to the other patients yet about Abby's untimely death.

Two crestfallen nurses agreed and then headed to Tony Conroy's room. As they stepped in the hall, instead of going to Tony's room, Rita stared at Natalie. "Let's run down and grab a pop or a cup of coffee. We have plenty of time and to tell you the truth, I could use a minute or two to collect myself before we go in and talk to Tony."

With a sigh, Natalie nodded her agreement at the suggestion. "I could use a break myself."

*   *   *

While the two women were headed to the cafeteria, Doctor Jonas Sullivan was surveying the mess in the bathroom attached to Abby Benson's hospital room. He turned

87

away from the horrific scene to look at Rex Corgin. "I need you to go downstairs and call the Portsmouth Police Department. Wait downstairs for them, I'll stay in here and keep an eye on things."

Rex nodded, glad to be headed out of the room.

As soon as Jonas knew he was gone, the doctor reached in his pocket, pulled out his cell phone and dialed. When he heard the sound of Doctor Harrell's hello, Jonas sighed. "We have a problem Fredrick."

The dark blue eyes narrowed as Fredrick Harrell frowned, not liking the sound of Jonas' voice. "What's going on Jonas?"

As he began talking, Doctor Sullivan made his way back into the bathroom. "Abby Benson is dead. She just killed herself by cutting open her forearms. She got the main artery, there's blood everywhere."

The blue eyes grew wide. "How the hell did she find something to slice open her arms with?"

Reaching down, careful to avoid the blood, Doctor Sullivan picked up a half inch wide, two inch long, slightly curved item that was dark grey in color. He held the item up to get a better look at it. "It would seem our Abby found something rare and dangerous to use. It is also something she never should have had in her possession."

Jonas slipped the article in his pocket. "I need a substitute object to place in here with her. I don't want anyone seeing what she actually used. Rex Corgin is downstairs now calling the police. We don't have much time."

Fredrick Harrell nodded. "Don't worry, I'll bring something up."

As he hung up the phone, Doctor Sullivan looked over at Abby's crumpled body and shook his head. "Abby, why would you do this?"

Jonas shook his head and went out to stand by Abby's bed and wait for Fredrick to bring him some kind of weapon to plant on Abby. The doctor wasn't really worried about much of an investigation taking place. Still, he hoped whatever Doctor Harrell came up with was something you could use to not only slice your arm wide open, but something easily attainable.

*　　*　　*

In the cafeteria, Rita and Natalie had gotten their drinks and were seated at a table. Neither woman knew what to say and for a moment spent more time looking down at their drinks than at each other. Finally, Rita cleared her throat. "I'm sorry you had to see that Natalie. We've never had a death here since I've been on staff. Given the types of problems our patients have, I guess we've really been lucky. It's a hell of a way for you to start your first day though."

The head of dark blonde hair shook back and forth. "Don't worry about me. As a nurse, I know just how close death can be every day. Abby isn't the first suicide I've dealt with. I'm really sorry you lost your patient. As a nurse, I know how close you get to those you take care of."

Rita nodded. "With Abby's severe depression not responding to treatment, I feel I should have been watching her closer. I wish I could have done something, anything to stop this from happening."

Reaching across the table, Natalie took Rita's hand. "The fact that you feel that way shows how much you care. I'm sure Abby knew that."

Staring at Natalie, brown eyes moist, Rita sighed. "I hope so."
She pushed back her chair and stood up from the table. "Let's go see Tony. The best thing I can do is keep myself busy."

As the two women headed back upstairs, they could hear the sound of sirens headed toward Whitmore Hills. Neither feeling like talking to law enforcement just yet, Rita and Natalie hurried to Tony's room, both noticing Abby's door remained closed as they passed by.

Using her key card, Rita opened Tony's door and the two woman stepped in. Natalie was thankful the door closing behind her shut out the sounds of the sirens. She held the clipboard to her chest with both hands, hoping the tight grip she held it with would stop the slight trembling of her hands.

Instead of sitting on his bed, Tony Conroy was in a chair at the small round table in his room. The set that included a table and two chairs was positioned only a few feet from the doorway Natalie and Rita had just entered through. Seeing the women, Tony stood. "Hey Rita, aren't you early today. I just finished lunch not too long ago. I thought you always saved the best patient for last."

Rita smiled. "I always do Tony. Doctor Sullivan is taking care of one of my patients today, so you get an early visit."

Tony was nodding at Rita, but his green eyes were focused on Natalie. Seeing the look, Rita smiled. "Tony, this is Natalie. She's joining the nursing staff here, so you'll be seeing a lot more of her."

Smiling, Tony stepped over and held out his hand. Letting go of one side of the clipboard, Natalie shook the extended hand. "Hello Tony, I'm looking forward to being your nurse."

As Tony smiled, Natalie could see the golden streaks in the green eyes seemed to make them shine. "It's nice to meet you Natalie."
Tony motioned toward the table he had just stood from. "I'm afraid I only have two chairs. Why don't you ladies have a seat? I'll sit on the bed. Besides you have to check my vitals anyway, right?"

Natalie nodded. "Why don't I do that?"

Setting the clipboard on the table, Natalie went to the bathroom and unlocked the closet. As she looked at Tony's chart on the wall, she was surprised to see he only had one medication on his list. The muscle relaxer he took was only once a day and he didn't take it until much later. Probably during the shift she would be taking on.
As Natalie came back into the room, she was pleased to see Rita laughing at something Tony had said. The woman looked much better than she had down in the

cafeteria.

Natalie quickly checked Tony's temperature, blood pressure, pulse and oxygen, finding all within normal ranges. When she finished, she stored the equipment back in the closet and locked it up. Then she joined Rita at the table.

Looking at the list of questions for Tony, Natalie frowned at the first one. Since she didn't know hardly anything about any of the patient's yet, she had to figure that Doctor Sullivan and Doctor Harrell had their reasons behind the questions they wanted the nurses to ask. With a sigh, she started. "Tony, do you feel you are a better person than your parents? Is that why you refused to work at their businesses?"

The green eyes staring at Natalie now, seemed to darken as Tony frowned. "I am a better person than either of my parents. I refused to work for them because I couldn't handle their holier than thou attitude. My mom and dad don't care who they hurt or had to step on to get to the top. My grandfather is the one who did all the work to make the business a success. He worked himself into an early grave to assure my dad wouldn't have to do the same thing. Not that my dad or my mom appreciated any of the sacrifices grandpa made. They couldn't wait for him to die so they could take over his car lot. Now the two of them own five or six businesses and they can keep them."

Natalie was surprised at the harsh quality to Tony's voice. He must have noticed the look she gave him, because he ran both hands through his thick brown hair and smiled at Natalie. "Sorry about that, touchy subject. My parents don't see things on quite the same level as I do. I think if you are a success at whatever you do, it is your responsibility to give that back and help others. My parents don't care to help anyone but themselves."
Tony laughed. "Including me, it was my parents who arranged for my stay at Whitmore Hills. More because I was an embarrassment to them than to get me help."

Natalie looked down at her clipboard to see the next question followed the same subject line Tony was talking about. "Do you resent your parents for thinking you belong here?"

Looking down, Tony studied his hands a moment before looking up and staring at Natalie. The green eyes were back to normal and Natalie saw something in them that made her want to trust the man staring so intently at her.

Taking a deep breath, Tony shook his head. "Not really I guess. I can understand them thinking I was crazy. I'm sure a few of the stories I told them about my adventures must have scared the hell out of them." Tony laughed. "Not as much as living through those stories scared me. Their only answers to the tales I was telling was to say I either had to be hooked on drugs or delusional. I don't take drugs, never did, at least until I got here, so that left the other option and a commitment to Whitmore Hills."

Natalie nodded, surprised to find herself believing the man and wanting to know just what the adventures were that Tony spoke about. Natalie looked down and saw she only had two more questions left to be asked. She would have rather skipped the next on the list and moved to the last. She hesitated a moment before she stared in the mesmerizing green eyes. "What's the worst place you've ever been Tony?"

The man seated on the bed didn't answer right away, instead he seemed to be staring, distractedly at the wall just behind Natalie's head and seeing something neither Natalie nor Rita could see. After a few minutes, his eyes focused again and he stared at Natalie. "The worst place I ever saw was the world I escaped from when the cops found me and my parents deserted me. I don't have a name for the place. If I didn't know better I might say you could call it hell. I think this place was worse than hell. It was hot though and I could see the tops of the mountains that surrounded the area were throwing out fire. You could see streams of red flowing down like rivers of blood."

Tony frowned. "Did you ever watch old westerns on T.V. and there's an animal or even a man out dying in the desert?" Tony raised one arm in the air as he talked and moved it in a slow wide circle. "You're shown the buzzards just circling around, waiting for their target to get weak enough for them to go in and attack."

Tony waited for both Natalie and Rita to nod before he put down his arm and continued. "In this place, the birds did that. Only they weren't like any vulture you've ever seen. Those things, whatever hell created them, were bigger than a man. They circled like those vultures though. I watched four of them do that. On the ground below them, an animal was in trouble. The thing had six legs, but at least two of them were broken. The animal half walked, half crawled across the red dirt. As I watched it, I was afraid to go help, not knowing if the animal was friendly or vicious. Suddenly, those damn flying creatures swooped down. One of them had these long gray claws that clamped down on that animals neck. While it held the creature immobile, the others attacked. I could hear the sound of snapping bones and then those things tore that animal apart and feasted on the remains in front of my eyes. For a minute or two, I was frozen to my spot. Then, knowing I could easily be their next prey, I turned away looking for a place to run. When I did that, I kicked a rock and made enough noise that I caught their attention. I saw all four heads turn as one to stare at me. Their black lifeless eyes made my heart jump to my throat. That's when I started running, not bothering to look back. I didn't need to, I could hear the sound of their enormous wings flapping in the dry, hot air. Then I felt one of those thing's claws. It burned like a hot knife as it ripped through the shirt I wore and sliced down my back. The pain was excruciating. I don't know of anything I could even compare that agony to, so you could understand."

Tony's words were almost running together, like the story he recalled was as painful as the claws that had ripped into his back and maybe by telling it quickly, the hurt would be less. He stopped talking a moment as he took a deep ragged breath.

"That's when I saw the tear that would lead me into the doorway and hopefully an escape. As I ran through, I landed in an alley. Someone must have seen me with my clothes torn and bloody and called the cops. A week later, I joined the patient list here at Whitmore Hills. I think my parents probably pulled a few strings to have that happen so fast. I guess I should be grateful to them for placing me here and not letting me rot in a jail cell somewhere."

As Tony finished telling the story he didn't look at either Natalie or Rita. He knew Rita had listened before to his explanation of not only that strange world, but a couple others as well. She'd never expressed either belief or disbelief in his tales. For Tony, Rita's neutrality was okay and something he could live with, but he hoped Natalie wouldn't just see his rantings of a bizarre world as delusional. For some reason he felt a connection with the new nurse and waited in anticipation for what her reaction would be.

Watching Tony, Natalie could see his agitation as he'd told the story, but she had also heard and felt something in his words that made her want to dismiss the diagnosis of Tony being delusional. Natalie was also thinking back to earlier when Megan's retelling of her nightmare seemed eerily similar to Tony's story. She stared at Tony now, almost willing him to look at her. A few moments later he did and Natalie could see the almost pleading look in his eyes, expressing a need for confirmation that she believed the words he had spoken. With Rita sitting next to her, Natalie didn't want to come right out and say the story sounded true. She hoped Tony could read her feelings on her face and in her eyes. Looking at Tony, Natalie nodded slightly and smiled. "I'm sorry you went through that Tony." Natalie sighed, hoping Rita didn't take her words as a confirmation of Tony's story. At the same time, she was hoping that was exactly what Tony perceived from her look. Seeing the green eyes light up, Natalie thought her intentions had worked. Tapping her pen on the clipboard, Natalie gladly asked the final question. "Could you also tell me about the best place you've ever seen?"

As Tony's head bobbed enthusiastically, Natalie could easily see this was a story that Tony was glad to remember.

"If the place I just talked about could be called hell, then the best place I've ever been to could easily be mistaken for Heaven."

Natalie noticed Tony used the phrase 'the best place I've ever been' and not just the best place he'd seen. She wondered if Rita had heard the difference in his wording. It was funny, but Natalie felt like she didn't care what Rita might be thinking just then. In fact, listening to Tony, Natalie felt like the two of them were alone in the room. She couldn't wait until she had her own shift when she could talk to Tony without Rita's presence. As she stared at Tony she saw the green eyes had become dreamy, like he was actually seeing something from his past.

His voice was lighthearted as he spoke. "The place was beyond beautiful. If I was an artist, I might be able to give you a better description. The mountains, the sky and the large lake there vied with each other with the most amazing shades of blue. The sand of the beach by the lake had a sparkle to it, like tiny pearls were imbedded in the sand.

The sand seemed to line up with the grass.
Not grass like you'd see outside. The green
was a different shade than I've ever seen
before and when I knelt down to touch the
grass it felt like silk. The air was quiet and
as I drew in a breath, my lungs filled with
sweet fresh air. The oxygen level must have
been higher than what I was used to,
because I felt slightly dizzy, even euphoric. I
could see people standing on the other side
of the lake, but the distance was too far for
me to see any detail. I wanted to head over
there, but I could hear my name being called
somewhere behind me. Reluctantly, I turned
to the sound that somehow compelled me to
move toward it and away from this
astounding place."
With a deep sigh, Tony shook his head.
"I've never been able yet to go back to the
doorway to that place. I've seen other places
close to it, but none ever quite matched what
I felt while I was there. Someday I'll go
there again and I have a feeling when I do,
I'll be there to stay."

As Tony finished speaking, the green eyes
darkened with sadness and loss. To Natalie,

Tony's story and his description of this special place sounded a lot like the picture that Steve said he wanted to paint. The one he had compared to Heaven. She smiled at Tony. "That sounds like a wonderful place Tony. I hope someday you do get the chance to go there again."

Hearing the sound of a sigh, Natalie turned to Rita as she realized that she and Tony weren't alone in the room.

Natalie smiled. "That's the last question on my list."

Rita nodded. "I think we're done here for today then."

She looked over at Tony. "Thanks for sharing your tales with us Tony. Natalie and I have to go get some computer work done, but we'll be back tomorrow and then Natalie will be taking over the four to midnight shift on her own."

Standing, Tony came over and shook Rita's hand first, thanking her for the visit, then he grabbed Natalie's hand and gave it a light squeeze as he smiled at her. The green eyes stared into the light brown ones and liked what he saw there. "It was nice to meet you Natalie. I think I'll enjoy your being my nurse."

Leaving Tony's room, Natalie followed Rita to the computer room where they recorded the day's events, leaving out the visit to Abby's room. Neither of them knowing just what they should put in the record. As they were finishing up, Rusty stepped in the room. Running a hand through his rust colored hair, Rusty shook his head. "I just heard about Abby, what a tragedy. I thought she was getting a little better. Does anyone know what she used to commit suicide? I mean, we keep anything even close to a possible weapon away from the patients."

Rita shook her head. "We haven't heard anything since we left Abby's room. Doctor Sullivan is taking care of everything. I'm more than happy to leave that mess in his hands. I feel awful, like I let her down."

Rusty slipped an arm around Rita's shoulder and then seeing Natalie's sad brown eyes, the free arm went around her shoulders too. "Both of you just need to go get some rest.

Maybe grab yourselves a glass of wine or a beer. Something like this could happen at any time. We all know our patients are walking a tightrope of emotions. Don't either of you feel guilty about any of this. I just hope the police don't get involved. The last thing we need is to have the law wandering around when we are trying to get our work done."

Rita nodded. "By the way, Doctor Sullivan requested we not share the news with the other patients right now. I think he might feel it would be better for him to break the news when he takes the patients for their monthly trip to the woods."

With a long sigh, Rusty nodded. "I don't have a problem with that, in fact I'd rather not share this awful news with the patients either. Like I said they all are dealing with their own troubles, they don't need any more to make things worse."

Rita and Natalie agreed and then left Rusty to his work as they headed to their apartments.

Chapter 6

A week later, Natalie felt like she was really fitting in well to her new job. After finishing out that week, she was thankful that no more dramatic incidents had occurred. Now, the two doctors had taken the four remaining patients with them for the overnight stay at Doctor Sullivan's cabin in the Holden National Forest that sat just behind Whitmore Hills.

Natalie was surprised that the doctors made the once a month trip. The nursing staff along with Arthur and the two security guards, Rex and Vann were all enjoying pizza they'd had delivered to the hospital's recreation room.

Natalie was thinking it was sad that the room was probably never enjoyed by the patients it was designed for. At Whitmore Hills, the patients only left their rooms during the once a month excursion they took into the woods.

Natalie was sitting at a table with Carl and Rita, while the rest of the employees were playing pool. Natalie was frowning. "What do the patients do on these trips they take?"

Rita shrugged. "I'm really not sure. Neither Doctor Sullivan nor Doctor Harrell add anything to the patient's records after they return either. I'm not even sure if the patients interact. I kind of feel like the trips are more for the doctors to spend personal time with the patients than for any other reason."

Carl was nodding. "The patients have never told me anything about those trips. I would think if they spent time visiting with each other they would tell me about it."
With a shrug, Carl lifted his mug and downed the contents. "Personally, I'm just happy all of us get to have the day off. I know I look forward to it every month and I think the others do too. I really appreciate the doctors not only letting us take over this room, but not minding that we bring in pizza and beer."

Natalie laughed. "I guess that is a plus."

Standing, Carl ran a hand through his blonde hair and then looked at the two women, blue eyes sparkling. "Who wants to try and beat me at a game of air hockey?"

Natalie shook her head, but Rita nodded and stood. "I'll take that challenge. Just remember you still owe me five bucks from a month ago when you bet me I couldn't beat you."

Carl laughed. "Okay, let's make it double or nothing. I'll even buy you a beer."

Rita playfully slapped the foot taller man's shoulder. "The beer's already paid for." She turned back to Natalie. "Are you sure you don't want to play?"

Shaking her head, Natalie leaned back in her chair. "No thanks, I'm happy to just sit here and relax."

As the two walked away, Natalie realized the last thing she was actually doing was relaxing. She couldn't stop thinking about the patients, especially Tony, spending an overnight stay in the woods. During the last week, Natalie already found herself looking forward to her visits with her last patient of the day. She usually hit Tony's room around nine thirty at night and spent an hour and a half with him, like she did the other patients. She got along with all the patients in her care, but with each visit to Tony Conroy's room, Natalie felt that special connection she had felt when they first met growing. After Tony had described the two worlds he'd seen to her on that first visit, he'd only talked about one other. That world was almost identical to the one they all lived in. Although everything recorded in Tony's medical chart showed him to be delusional, Natalie couldn't help but think Tony's recollections felt more like reality than not. There was just something about the man that made Natalie not only want to trust him, but also wanting to know him better. Not Tony as a patient, but Tony as a man.

The sound of Rusty's voice broke Natalie out of her reverie. "Hey, this is a party. You shouldn't be sitting here all alone."

Looking up, Natalie smiled. "Pull up a chair and sit down then."

Taking Natalie up on her offer, Rusty sat down and placing his elbows on the table, rested his head in his hands and stared at Natalie. "You were off in your own little world. Anything you'd like to talk about?"

With a shrug, Natalie sighed. "I was thinking about the patients. What do you think they do out in the woods?"

Rusty laughed. "I don't know and none of them are sharing either. Believe me, I was curious about that too. I've asked all of them that very question. All I've been able to get from any of them is a vague reply about the beauty and serenity of spending time out of the hospital. After hearing the same answer over and over again, I gave up asking. Now, I just focus on enjoying the time we all get off."

Natalie nodded, but she was thinking she couldn't wait to hear what Tony had to say about the short trip.

Natalie pushed the thoughts of Tony and the

other patients from her mind and joined her coworkers in their free night of playing games and spending time without the responsibility of patients.

After cleaning up the recreation room, everyone headed over to the apartment complex. After the good nights were all said, Natalie found herself alone in her apartment.

Changing into her nightgown, Natalie crawled into bed, but left the lamp on beside her bed. As her thoughts went back to Tony, Natalie knew she wouldn't be able to fall asleep any time soon. Instead of trying, she pulled a pen and a pad of paper out of the drawer and began writing down what she'd learned about Tony through a week of not only talking to the man, but searching through the file the hospital kept on him in the computer. A search through that file had shown, like her, Tony was an only child. His parents, Lance and Teresa Conroy, were, like Tony had said, the owners of several businesses that were doing extremely well financially. Tony had spent his life working several different jobs, none of them in the businesses his parents owned.

Tony had begun having sessions with psychiatrists at the age of thirteen, almost twenty years ago. Despite the diagnosis of being delusional with bouts of depression, this trip to Whitmore Hills was Tony's first stay at a psychiatric hospital. Other than the various doctor's diagnosis of him being delusional, nothing more had been stated in those records.

Natalie's heart went out to the thirteen year old boy. At thirteen, the biggest worry in her mind had been whether or not the boy she had her latest crush on would take her to whatever school dance was going on at the time. Tony had spent six years in college, receiving both a bachelor's degree in physics and one in geology and then a master's degree in computer science.

Natalie wished she would have known Tony then. Her own years at college had been spent mostly in her dorm room alone studying. She'd had several boyfriends through the years, but none had turned serious. In fact, Natalie felt in the last week, she'd spent more time thinking about Tony than she had any of the men she'd come in contact with through the years.

In her training as a nurse, Natalie had been warned against getting overly close to any of her patients. Any kind of romantic involvement was definitely frowned upon. As Natalie wrote down the few things she knew about Tony, she realized she was doing the one thing she'd been warned not to do. She just couldn't stop thinking about Tony or the way she felt as she gazed into his incredible green eyes.

If Tony was delusional, she was finding herself caught up in and believing the stories. She'd known men for years that didn't make her feel even close to the way Tony did and she'd only known him a week. Shaking her head, Natalie tore the page she'd been writing on out of the notebook and then ripped it to shreds.

Getting out of bed, she walked into the kitchen and dumped the shards of paper into the garbage can. She needed to get hold of herself. More than one psychiatrist had diagnosed Tony Conroy as delusional. She needed to remember that.

What was wrong with her, buying into the stories and accepting the tales as the truth? People didn't step through some kind of rip in the air and enter strange worlds.
It was just that those green eyes looked so sincere when Tony talked.

As Natalie headed back to her room, she shook her head and smiled at her foolishness. Reminding herself that Tony was the patient and she was the nurse. Her job was to help him stop having the delusions, not encourage them by believing the crazy stories Tony shared.

Natalie turned off the light and rolled over on to her side as she tried to find the rest she knew was going to be elusive.

Especially when she closed her eyes and the image of Tony filled her mind.

Chapter 7

As Natalie was getting ready to finish her rounds with her last patient of her shift, she smiled. It was almost June and she'd been at the hospital a month now.

Natalie had settled into her routine at Whitmore Hills and because she was seldom given the chance to go to town and spend the money she earned, her bank account balance was growing quickly.

She didn't have to worry about how she was going to make a rent payment while also trying to pay utilities like she had before she had landed this job.

All in all, she couldn't be happier about accepting the job at Whitmore Hills. There were a few strange rules, like not being allowed to go to town or having internet access at her apartment, but what job didn't have its downside?

Natalie smiled, thinking how nice it was to only have four patients to care for. Then she felt guilty thinking of Abby's suicide being the reason for the lowered patient count. Shaking that thought from her head, Natalie focused instead on the next room she was headed for, her last and most favorite patient in the hospital.

Using her key card, she unlocked Tony Conroy's door and stepped inside. As she did, Natalie frowned at the sight of Tony laying on his bed. He usually was seated at the table, eager for her company.

The two had gone beyond discussing the few questions Doctor Sullivan and Doctor Harrell compiled each day. Those questions were usually asked, answered and then recorded in the first ten minutes of Natalie entering the room. The rest of the hour and a half of Natalie's visit was spent talking about their past lives and their hopes for the future.

Tonight though, Tony's usual bright green eyes, looking over at Natalie, were dark and dejected looking.

Placing her clipboard on the table, Natalie stepped quickly to the side of Tony's bed. "What's wrong Tony? Did something happen?"

The green eyes stared at Natalie for what felt like an eternity before Tony moved to a sitting position and shook his head.
"The trip is the day after tomorrow. I don't want to go."

Natalie sat on the bed beside Tony. They had never talked about the trips the doctors took the patients on. Although the upcoming trip would only be the second since Natalie had begun working at Whitmore Hills. She'd been curious about the reasoning behind them and dying to know what happened in the cabin in the woods. She'd also been almost afraid to ask Tony. She'd asked the other nurses who were clueless about anything to do with the trips. They always seemed perfectly happy not knowing about the ventures.

Now, Natalie took a deep breath before she asked the question that had been on her mind for almost a month. "What happens on those trips Tony? Why don't you want to go?"

A puzzled look covered Tony's face as he shook his head. "I'm not sure."

Now it was Natalie who had the confused look. "What do you mean, you're not sure? You spend a lot of time at that place, you're even there over night. You must know what happens. Do you just sit in the cabin or do you get to go out into the woods?"

The eyebrows drew down over the green eyes as Tony shrugged. "It feels like a dream that fades away the more you try to remember it. I can see all of us sitting in the white hospital van. No one's talking, but we're all gawking at each other. I look from face to face, wondering why these people are in a psychiatric hospital like me. To me they look normal."

Tony laughed. "Whatever that looks like."

He turned away from Natalie as he spoke, his voice sounding almost robotic.

"We drive through the trees. They're so close they scrape against the sides of the van. I can hear the screech of branches against the glass. I don't know how long we drive. I'm just caught up in the landscape we're passing through and then we're stopping in front of the cabin. It looks old and stands beneath a shelter of trees. Doctor Sullivan and Doctor Harrell escort us inside. Once we're settled on four of the six chairs in the living room, Doctor Sullivan builds a fire. I can remember hearing the sound of the cracking and popping of the wood as it burns. I'm almost mesmerized by the leaping flames. So much so that the sound of Doctor Sullivan talking is more like a whisper in my mind."

Tony shook his head. "That's it, that's what I remember. The next thing I know, it is already morning and I'm back here and stuck in this room."

Natalie frowned. "So why are you so upset about going back? Nothing you just said gives a reason for that."

Turning back to look at Natalie, Tony shook his head. "I wish I knew. First of all, something's wrong that I can't remember. Once a month we make that trip. I've been here a long time Natalie. You'd think by now I'd remember more than that. I have dreams though, after we return. Dreams of standing in the other worlds that I've told you about. I'm not alone in the dreams though. Other people are with me, I think they're the other patients. This last time after we came back, I had those dreams, but one of those patients wasn't with me any longer. I don't know any of the other patient's names. The woman who's missing from my dreams is a tiny lady. Maybe only five foot tall with dark hair and eyes. Do you know who she is?"

The sound of Natalie's gasp answered Tony's question. He frowned. "Who is she Natalie?"

Covering her mouth with her hand, Natalie felt sick. She shook her head and removed the hand. "Not is, was. Abby Benson committed suicide just before your last trip.

Didn't Doctor Sullivan tell you?"

As Tony shook his head, Natalie felt her anger rise. "He asked us not to tell you. He said he'd take care of letting you know. Why the hell didn't he tell you?"

Tony shrugged. "I don't know, but at least that explains why she's missing from my dreams."

Staring at Tony, Natalie frowned. "Tony, none of that makes sense. Why would any of the others be in your dreams and how could Abby's suicide make her absent from the dreams you've been having? You didn't even know her name or that she was dead."

Tony stared at Natalie. "I'm not crazy."

Natalie grabbed Tony's hand. "I know you're not, I've known that since the first day I met you. I still don't understand how the trips to the cabin once a month and you're dreams could be related."

Tony looked down at where Natalie's hand held his own. "I have a theory about that. It sounds really crazy though. I'm afraid if I tell you what I think, you'll think I deserve to not only be in a psychiatric hospital but that I should be here for an extended stay."

Natalie shook her head. "I know better than that Tony. Tell me your theory. At least I can try to give you my opinion on your thoughts."

Tony hesitated for just a minute and then nodded. "Okay, here goes. I think when the doctors take us patients to the cabin they somehow force me to take the others with me to those other worlds. That's why I find them joining me in my dreams or I guess a better description would be my nightmares. Anyway, I really feel the dreams are my subconscious mind remembering the reality of what happened at that cabin. I have no recollection of any of it when I am awake, but in my sleep, it's all there."

Natalie frowned. "You said before you step through some kind of tear to get to the other worlds. I don't understand what you mean by that."

The green eyes opened wide. "You've never seen them?"

Natalie shook her head. "I don't know anyone, besides you, that does."

Tony smiled and grasped Natalie's hand in a tighter grip, thankful that she sounded like she believed that he had seen those tears. "Did you ever drive down the highway on a warm day and look on the road ahead of you and see the distortion in the air caused by the heat waves?"

Tony waited for Natalie's nod before he continued. "The tears look like that. If you don't know what you're looking for, they could easily be dismissed as a figment of your imagination or a similar distortion caused by heat or some other anomaly. I saw the first one when I was thirteen. I didn't dismiss the irregularity. Instead I stepped through. Later, in college, I did a lot of research. Our world is covered by magnetic lines, when they cross in just the right way, that crossing makes a rip in the atmosphere that creates an opening. That is the tear between worlds."

Tony stared at Natalie waiting for the look he'd seen so many times, the look of disbelief. When the look didn't come, he let out a sigh of relief and allowed a brief smile to make its way to his face.

Then, Natalie frowned. "How does one of these openings explain the other patients being in your dreams or your lack of memory about your trips to the cabin?"

Taking a deep breath, Tony shrugged. "I have a second part to my theory that might be the answer to explain everything, but it's even harder to believe."
Then he laughed. "I guess not any harder to believe than an opening between worlds."

As Tony walked Natalie through his theory, at first she felt he had to be way off target, but the more she thought about it, the more it made sense.

When Tony finished, Natalie stared at him. "Why would Doctor Sullivan and Doctor Harrell do something like that? What do you think they would be looking for in the other worlds?"

Tony shrugged. "It's hard to say. If they asked me, and told me why they wanted to go, I'd probably just tell them how to get to the other worlds."

Then Tony shook his head. "Then again, maybe not. After all, they're keeping me here with a diagnosis of being delusional and apparently with no cure for my psychiatric problem, they plan on just keeping me here."

Natalie nodded and then frowned. "How are you ever going to be able to prove this theory of yours?"

Tony shrugged. "I have an idea about that, but I need your help and I think it's too dangerous to even have you try."

Natalie's mouth straightened in a grim line. "Maybe you should tell me your idea and let me decide if I think it's too chancy."

Staring at Natalie, Tony was undecided. If he told Natalie what he wanted to do, she'd agree, despite the risk. He wasn't sure if he could live with that. What if she got hurt? In the last month of Natalie's daily hour and a half visits, Tony had fallen in love with the woman. He had no idea if Natalie felt the same. He knew Natalie didn't talk to him the same way Rita did when she visited. The two of them were still just nurse and patient and although Tony would love their relationship to be more, he didn't know if their relationship could go anywhere with them stuck in the roles they were in right now and in this hospital.

Natalie reached up and gently stroked the side of Tony's face. "We need to find out what's really happening Tony, for you and for the other patients. Please, tell me what your plan is."

The sensation of Natalie's touch sent a shiver through Tony's body. Looking in her eyes, he could tell she felt something too. Reaching up, Tony covered Natalie's hand with his own and nodded. "Okay, but if you feel any trepidations about my idea, promise me you'll say no. The last thing I want to do is put you in danger."

Natalie smiled. "I promise."

Tony drew in a deep breath before pulling Natalie's hand from his face but continuing to hold on to it. "When the doctors take all of us patients on the trip to the cabin, you'd have to follow us. You'd have to make sure you're not seen by anyone here or by any of the patients that will be going to the cabin in the van. I don't know how they'd react seeing you outside the hospital atmosphere. Once we arrive at the cabin, you'd have to find a way to watch and see what the doctors are doing. If they're doing what I think they are, I want you to leave and get back here. I don't want you to confront them. All I want to do is get confirmation that my theory is right. If you're seen, anything could happen. You probably don't know this, but the nurse whose job you have now also believed I was telling the truth about the other worlds and now she's gone."

Natalie shook her head. "I was told Shelley Morris quit and probably went to live with her family in Florida."

Tony shrugged. "I really hope that's what happened. I liked her, Shelley was a nice lady. Maybe it's just a strange coincidence that she believed me and then disappeared. Either way, I thought you should know and it's probably not a good idea to let it slip that you don't think I'm crazy."

Tony smiled.

"I mean, if that is how you feel."

Leaning over, Natalie kissed Tony's cheek. "I don't think you're crazy and I want to try your plan."

Tony's face grew serious as he nodded and turned so he could change the kiss he had received on his cheek into a much longer one that took them both by surprise in its intensity and also took both of their breaths away with the passion that came with it.

Pulling back, Natalie's eyes widened. "Wow, why did we wait so long to try that?"

Shaking his head, Tony smiled. "I don't know, but it was worth the wait."

Natalie laughed. "That it was and I'd like to hang around for a few more, but I better go get my work done and get out of here before someone starts getting suspicious about me being in your room so long."

She gave Tony one more quick kiss. "We can talk more tomorrow night and then you can plan on me finding a way to follow that hospital van. We need to find out what's really going on."

Tony nodded and then watched as Natalie grabbed her clipboard and left his room, blowing him a kiss on the way out.

As Natalie went downstairs to the computer room, she realized she hadn't even asked Tony one question from the list.

Sitting down, she hurriedly filled in made up answers and then began transferring the information from all four of her patients to their files. The sound of laughter startled her and she jumped before turning toward the doorway.

Vann Shields was leaning against the door frame, blue eyes staring at Natalie. "Looks like someone is breaking a cardinal rule and getting involved with one of her patients."

Natalie frowned. "What are you talking about Vann?"

Pointing at the screens that sat above Natalie's head, Vann smiled. "Did you forget we record everything?"

Natalie felt like she'd been slapped. "Oh hell, it's not what you think Vann. To me, Tony is more than just a patient. Sometimes you can't help how your heart feels. Some things can't be stopped once they begin. Neither Tony or I expected to feel this way."

Vann smiled and ran a hand over his bald head. "Believe me, I understand what you're saying, but I don't think the doctors will. I can scramble the video for those few minutes. I don't have a way to erase the pictures but the screen will be so distorted, no one will be able to tell what the original image was."

Natalie stared wide eyed at Vann. "Would you really do that?"

Vann nodded. "I'll be glad to, we employees need to stick together. Besides, you never know when I might need a favor and I wouldn't want anyone to say I stood in the way of love in the making."

Standing, Natalie moved over and hugged Vann. "Whatever you need, all you have to do is ask, and it's yours. Thanks Vann, you're a life saver."

Vann smiled. "I don't know about that, but you're welcome. I'll take care of it as soon as you finish up in here."

Natalie hurriedly finished putting in the information, seeing something in the files she knew would be useful and then headed home reminding herself she needed to be a lot more careful in the future.

Chapter 8

While the rest of her co-workers headed to the hospital's recreation room as soon as the van left carrying the doctors and their patients, Natalie pleaded a terrible headache and stayed home. It had taken an incredible amount of acting and pleading on her part, but Natalie had finally convinced the others she was just planning on a long rest to sleep away the pain.

Looking out the window of her apartment, she saw the others disappear into the hospital and then waited another hour before she pulled out the map she'd been able to print out from the hospital's computer. It showed the location of Doctor Sullivan's cabin.

Both Natalie and Tony had been relieved when Natalie had found it after she'd left Tony's room the night before last and after she'd had the encounter with Vann.

Natalie had been worried about trying to follow the hospital's van without being seen and finding the map had been a major release of that worry anyway. She had plenty more to keep her anxiety high. Even now, with the map in hand, she could feel the palpitations of her heart as she waited for the right time to leave her apartment.

She'd have to take her car and worried one of her co-workers would see her and come running out to question what she was doing. Natalie had tried to think of excuses just in case that happened. She discarded each as lamer than the next. She crossed her fingers, hoping none of that would happen.

Dressed in black clothes, Natalie walked out to her car and slid in behind the wheel, feeling like a criminal.

She backed her car out, her eyes glued on the hospital building, waiting for the doors to slam open and someone to come running out.

When that didn't happen, Natalie let out her breath and focused on driving on the overgrown path that had at one time passed for a road. Following the map she had procured, Natalie drove to what she hoped was only a few blocks away from and walking distance to the cabin. She parked her car in a grove of trees, hoping her hiding place was good enough.

Stepping out of the car, Natalie thought about trying to break off a few branches and covering her vehicle. She dismissed the idea. If she needed to make a quick getaway, she didn't want her vision obscured by the branches and didn't think she'd have the time to remove them.

Natalie made her way toward the cabin. She stopped every few feet to hide behind the trees as she walked. Her process was walk a few feet, hide behind a tree and then making sure the coast was clear, repeat the procedure. By the time she saw the cabin, it was beginning to get dark and Natalie felt her chances of not being seen were greatly improved by the absence of light.
She needed to get close enough to try and

hear what was going on, or even better, find a window she could peek into.

Running up behind a tree, Natalie stole a look from behind her hiding place and her breathing stopped seeing how close she was. For one brief second, she contemplated the idea of just turning around and running back to her car to make her way back to the safety of her apartment, or even better, driving in the opposite direction and just keep going until she got as far away from this nightmare as possible. The thought of the doctors in the cabin, doing God knew what to Tony, a man she had come to love, drove the thought from her mind.

Natalie's eyes roamed the front of the cabin, searching for any clue that might indicate the best place for her to head. The windows were covered with curtains and all looked dark. As she stared at the building, she caught a glimmer of light. It wasn't a steady glow and she thought of Tony telling her about the fire he had watched while sitting in the cabin.

Hoping that's where he was now, Natalie

drew in a breath and ran to the corner of the cabin that was closest to the window. Dropping to the ground, Natalie crawled over until she was almost beneath the window. She slid in behind a bush, ignoring the scratches to her exposed hands and face. Then she sat down, pulled her knees in close to her chest and waited.

She was just about to give up and try for a better location when she heard a voice she recognized as belonging to Doctor Jonas Sullivan.

"Do you think enough time has elapsed yet?"

A laugh could be heard and then the answering voice of Doctor Fredrick Harrell was heard. "Hell yes, look at the four of them. They were so out of it on the bus from the sedation, I worried how we were going to manage dragging them in here. Go ahead and start."

When Doctor Sullivan's voice could be heard again, Natalie was surprised at the change. Now the voice that had sounded anxious just moments before was calm and soothing. "Just watch the fire. The flames are making you sleepy. With each flicker your eyes are growing heavy. Everything is okay, go ahead and rest. You'll need all of your strength later, but for now just close your eyes and rest. You're all doing fine, just close those eyes. Go ahead and rest."

Natalie was holding her breath. Afraid that even the slightest sound of her breathing might be heard by the men in the room just on the other side from where she sat. Realizing that was the wrong thing to be doing, Natalie slowly let out the air, careful to do it without making a noise.
The patients must have succumbed to the suggestion given because now Doctor Sullivan and Doctor Harrell could be heard conversing with each other.

Doctor Sullivan's voice was the first Natalie heard followed by Doctor Harrell's reply.

"We'll let them rest a couple of hours. By then the drugs will have worn off. I can keep them hypnotized while we send them out to find an opening."

"Do you think there are more around here Jonas? The patients have already been to quite a few doorways and so far we've only found a few substances that are going to be useful to us."

Natalie heard a grunt.

"Those few samples we've gotten are already proving to be well worth the time and effort we are expending. Don't worry Fredrick, Tony will find a split and take the others through. If we can just find a few more plants from these strange worlds, I know we can come up with amazing drugs. No one else has the capabilities we do using that vegetation and there is no way for anyway to duplicate our experiments. Not only will we both be rich, but our names will go down in history for our good works in advancing medicine."

Natalie didn't like the sound of Doctor Harrell's laughter that followed the words Doctor Sullivan had just stated.
She started to stand, ready to run into the cabin and put a stop to whatever the doctors were planning. Remembering her promise to

Tony, Natalie gritted her teeth in frustration. Her fists clenched so tightly her fingernails were digging into the palms of her hands.

Drawing in slow breaths, Natalie finally got herself under control. It would be a mistake to run inside. She wouldn't be any help to Tony or the other patients, especially if she ended up missing like Shelley Morris had.

Crawling back out from her hiding place behind the bush, Natalie reluctantly made her stealthy retreat away from the cabin and back through the woods to her car.

Once inside her vehicle, Natalie sat for five minutes as all that she'd just heard back at the cabin ran through her mind. Tony's theory had been right. He had shared with Natalie his suspicions that he and the others had been hypnotized. Now she had the proof, but where to go from here was a question she had no answer for.

The hooting sound of an owl, made Natalie's heart skip a beat and brought her mind back to the present. She needed to get

back to her apartment before she was
discovered spying here or absent there.

She made the drive almost mechanically.
Her mind on everything but the path she was
driving on.
As Natalie pulled into the apartment
complex, she noticed that all the apartments
were dark. Looking toward the hospital, she
could see plenty of lights blazing and hoped
that meant her fellow employees were all
still inside and enjoying their night off.

Going into her place, Natalie left the lights
off, not wanting anyone to think she was
awake and stopping by to check on her.
As she walked to her bedroom, she made her
way over and sat on her bed.

Putting her face in her hands, Natalie shook
her head despairingly. All she could do now
was wait and worry, that and hope Tony
would be back safely in the morning.
Even then, she didn't want to go to the
hospital to check on him until her normal
shift started and that wasn't until four P.M.

Removing her hands and lifting her head, Natalie sat up straight. The light brown eyes narrowed as she thought about the doctor's lab in the hospital's basement. That was the only logical place for them to keep any samples the patients brought back from the other worlds. If she waited until her co-workers returned from the night in the recreation room, then only one guard should be on duty at the hospital, if that. For all she knew, no one stayed on guard. Why would they with no patients to watch?

Nodding at the thought, Natalie smiled. Getting up, she went to her closet and dug out her camera.

Then she returned to sit and wait for the sound of her co-workers headed back to their apartments.

Chapter 9

In the cabin, Doctor Sullivan was standing in front of the four seated patients. All had their eyes closed, awaiting his instructions. Jonas Sullivan grinned, but his grey eyes held no light. He liked the power he felt having four lives under his control. All it took was a suggestion he'd planted in their minds to put them in this altered state that had been caused using hypnosis.

Jonas turned at the sound of Fredrick Harrell clearing his throat. "We really need to get started Jonas."

The dark head bobbed and Jonas once again focused the grey eyes on his patients. "It's time for all of you to focus on the fire." When Jonas said the word fire, the four sets of eyes opened and the heads turned to stare at the dancing flames. "That's right, just think of the burning flames. Tony, you are going to be in charge of the others. You will find an opening and lead them through. All of you will be responsible for bringing back at least one specimen. You've done this before. Look for plants that can be placed in the buckets you will all be carrying. If you see anything else that looks interesting and that could be useful you may add it to your bucket. When you've all obtained your samples you will then return here for further directions. If you understand your instructions, nod your heads."

Jonas waited for the nods before he continued.

"That's good, you're all doing fine. Now, please stand and we can go outside to get the equipment you will be using on your journey."

Without speaking to the doctors, the four patients walked single file out the cabin door behind Jonas and into the dark night. Fredrick Harrell followed behind Ted who was at the back of the line.

Once outside, Jonas handed each patient a bucket and a small shovel. He moved to stand in front of Tony. "I want you to find an opening to a doorway that the four of you haven't been to previously. Once you are inside, it will be your job to keep the others on task. You've done all of this before and know what is expected of you. Go inside, gather what you need quickly and then return through the same entrance and come back here to Doctor Harrell and myself. If you understand all you need to do is nod."

As soon as Tony's head began its downward move, Jonas was already smiling and rubbing his hands together. "I suggest you get started then."

Tony's head swiveled from side to side as he scanned the wooded area, green eyes squinting in search of the split in the air. In a few moments he smiled and pointed before turning to the other patients. "Over there, just beside that big pine tree."
Tony started walking and the others followed dutifully behind.

Jonas and Fredrick followed the small group, staying just a few steps behind them. They wanted to mark the spot where Tony had found that special tear between the worlds.

As Tony led the others through and all disappeared. Jonas turned to Fredrick. "I guess the waiting begins."

Stepping back from the place no longer visible. Jonas pointed over to a piece of turned over ground. "Is that where we buried Shelley Morris?"

Staring over at the spot, Fredrick shrugged. "I think so, I'm surprised the grave hasn't been dug up by the wildlife out here. It would seem we do good work."

Jonas smiled and then leaned against a tree to wait for the return of his patients.

*   *   *

As soon as Tony stepped into the world, he knew it was one he hadn't been to before.

He also knew, looking around, it wasn't going to be too hard to find plants to retrieve. The moist landscape was covered in a variety of green plants, most so dark from water saturation they looked more black than green in color. Even the air felt like the small crew had just missed a heavy rain shower and the moisture was lingering behind. Tony turned to the taller of the two men. "I'm sorry, but I can't remember your name."

Steve smiled. "That's okay, I don't know anyone's name but yours and that's only because I heard the doctor say it. I'm Steve, where the hell are we?"
Steve pointed at the orange colored sun. "Weren't we just standing in the dark?"

Tony nodded. "The times are as different as the worlds themselves. I'm afraid I don't have a name to give you Steve. We're just in an alternate dimension and I don't think I want to stay here too long. The air feels awfully heavy to me. Why don't you help the lady and I'll have the other guy. We can hurry and get those samples. Just make sure

we all get different varieties."
Turning, Tony looked at the other two people in the group. "It would help if I knew your names."

Ted smiled and stuck out his hand. "I'm Ted. Nice to meet you."

Tony shook the hand and then turned to look at the only woman in their group. She didn't smile or offer her hand. "I'm Megan and I don't like being here."
Her head turned side to side nervously. "This place is strange. Look around, not one building or even a road that might eventually lead to one."

Tony shook his head. "Never mind, we won't be here long. Steve can help you pick out a plant and dig it up. I'll help Ted and then we can all get out of here. Just stay where we can see each other. I don't want anyone wandering away. From the looks of this place, we won't need to go far to dig up four plants."

The look on Megan's face was still one of indecision, but she nodded and followed

Steve a few feet away to a patch of green plants with purple streaks in the leaves. Tony and Ted stepped off in the opposite direction and began digging up their own specimens. The two had just put their plants in the buckets when they heard Megan scream. As Tony turned to stare in that direction, he realized it was actually Steve, not Megan who was in trouble. Steve was shaking his hand, trying to knock something off. Finally Tony saw what looked like an enormous black spider drop to the ground. Running over, he stepped on the thing. Then using the shovel he'd been digging with Tony scooped up the dead creature and dumped it in the pail next to the plant he'd put in there. Once that was done, Tony stared at Steve. "Let me look at your hand. Did that thing bite you?"

Holding up his hand, already beginning to swell, Steve nodded. "Hell yes it bit me. My hand is already starting to go numb." Steve flexed his fingers. "Damn, what was that thing?"

Tony shook his head. "I don't know, but the thing is dead now. We'll take it back with us. I'm sure the doctors will know what to do. Let's get the hell out of here. We have what we came for."

Steve nodded, lifting his bucket with his uninjured hand and sliding the one that had been bitten under that arm, hoping that putting pressure on it would ease the pain.

Tony walked over to a spot that looked like nothing but air to the others and pointed. "That's our way home."

The others frowned, but trusting Tony moved to where he had pointed and taking a step crossed into the woods through a split none of them had been able to see.
For a moment, they let their eyes adjust to a world twice as dark as the bright one they had just come from.
Doctor Sullivan stepped forward to greet the small group. "That didn't take long. Let's get back to the cabin with those samples."

Tony stepped forward. "Not so fast. Steve got bit by something over there. You need to take a look at his hand."

Tony held up his bucket. "I killed the thing and threw it in here."

Steeping over to Steve, Doctor Sullivan pointed at Steve's hand still under his arm. Setting down his pail first, Steve then gently pulled his hand out from under his arm and swung it toward the doctor. The hand had swelled to twice its normal size and was a mottled mixture of blue and red.

Taking Steve's hand, the doctor pressed down on the flesh. Steve winced and pulled back, beads of sweat covering his forehead. He wiped them off with his uninjured hand. "It hurts like hell and I'm burning up. You need to do something."

Staring at Steve, the doctor nodded. "We head back to the cabin and put you by the fire."

As before, as soon as the Doctor said the word fire, all four patients' eyes glazed over and they nodded. Doctor Sullivan looked over at Doctor Harrell. "Let's get these samples back to the cabin where we can get them put away."

Fredrick frowned and pointed at Steve's hand. "What about that?"

Jonas shrugged. "Not much we can do out here. Let's just focus on getting everyone back inside the cabin."

After tromping through the woods, the group entered the cabin. First the doctors had the patients put the buckets of plant samples in the kitchen, then they escorted the patients into to the living room.
Once all were seated, Doctor Sullivan began giving them directions.

"Just relax and watch the fire. The flames are beautiful, but they are making you tired. Feel how heavy your eyes are becoming. You need rest, your body is craving it. You're so tired, you need to sleep. Stand up and head into the bedroom. Your beds are ready and waiting for you. All you want to do right now is lay down and rest."

The four stood and turned away from the fire. Then they headed to one of the cabin's two bedrooms where four cots had been set up. Each contained a pillow and an old thin blanket. The doctors helped the patients to find their beds and lie down. It only took a few minutes before the doctors, assured the patients were asleep, headed to the kitchen to see what treasures the group had brought back for them.

Doctor Harrell went to the bucket Tony had been carrying first. Using the shovel he lifted out the dead bug. The insect was five inches across and had four long legs. "What should we do with this?"

Jonas Sullivan shrugged. "Just put it in a container, we can add it to our collection, you never know when it might come in useful."

Reaching up in one of the cupboards, Fredrick pulled out a lidded container. Taking off the lid, he dropped in the bug, a look of disgust on his face. "What about Steve? This thing bit him and he didn't look good."

Jonas shook his head. "We can worry about him later when I wake all the patients up. Right now, all I'm worried about is getting these plants into containers so we can move them out to the van."

Four hours later, their precious cargo moved to the van, the doctors stepped into the cabin's bedroom. Doctor Harrell moved over to the cot where Steve was laying. He frowned at Steve's ashen color. As he reached down to touch Steve's neck, the doctor already knew he wasn't going to find a pulse. He turned back to stare at Jonas. "He's dead, what the hell are we supposed to do now? We can't head back to the hospital with a dead body."

Jonas shrugged. "We've dealt with dead bodies before. We'll take him out to the woods and bury him. No one will be too surprised when we tell them Steve Lincoln went crazy out here and then ran off. I'll even add that story into the other patients' subconscious when I wake them and put in the hypnotic suggestions I always do. You worry too much Fredrick. C'mon, let's get that body out of here. We need to get back to the hospital."

The two men grabbed Steve's body and carried him into the woods not too far from where Shelley Morris lay in her own final resting place. Dropping Steve's body on the ground, Jonas went back to the cabin to grab two shovels. When he brought them back, Jonas and Fredrick dug a hole and rolled Steve's body into it, then filled the hole in.

When they finished the makeshift grave, the two men returned to the cabin and Doctor Sullivan stepped into the bedroom where the three patients left were still sleeping. "Time to get up, the fire is out. All of you wake up."

The three patients sat up on their cots and stared at the doctor. Jonas grinned, but like before, his grey eyes remained dark. "We're going back to the hospital. You all enjoyed your overnight stay at the cabin. The fire was mesmerizing and lovely to watch. You were happy for the rest and just glad to be out of your hospital rooms for a while."

Jonas stopped speaking long enough to let out a sigh. "Sadly, your fellow patient Steve had an extreme delusional episode and despite the valiant efforts of Doctor Harrell and myself we couldn't stop him from escaping. This unfortunate incident has only made you realize how lucky you are to be receiving good treatment in the safety of your hospital rooms. When I count to three, you will only remember what I just told you and nothing more about this trip. At that time you will get up and go outside to take your places in the van for the trip back to the hospital."

Doctor Sullivan took a deep breath and held it for a moment before letting it out slowly and then counting. "One… two… three. Okay, it's time, let's all go take our places in the van."

The three patients stood and slowly made their way to the van. Before they stepped in they were searched. Doctor Sullivan had been worried since Abby had used the claw from another world to kill herself. Satisfied nothing was being brought back, the patients were allowed to take their seats for the trip back to the hospital.

Chapter 10

At the same time Tony and the others were
headed to the other world, Natalie was
headed into the hospital and the basement
laboratory. She didn't know if the guards
were on duty, but as she made her way down
the set of stairs that led to the basement, she
was relieved to not see anyone.

Before she had headed over to the hospital,
Natalie had found a small flashlight and put
it in her pocket. As she stepped in the
basement and opened the first door she came
to, she realized her worries about having
enough light to see by had been
unnecessary. In the large room she had
stepped into, the several glass cases sitting
on the shelves all had lights in them. Besides
that lighting, almost every one of the
numerous plants in the room had a lamp
hanging above it. Natalie thought they were

the kind that gardeners used to help with plant growth. Ignoring the plants, Natalie moved over to see what the cases held.

The first one she stepped up to made her frown. The contents of the case consisted of two black rocks, one slightly larger than the other. The smaller one was only about the size of her fist.

Lifting her hand, Natalie placed her palm against the side of the glass. Her eyes grew large as the rocks inside began to glow with a bright turquoise tinted light.

She pulled her hand back and the light faded. Natalie moved her hand to the glass and then pulled it away several times, watching the light as it seemed to pulse with the movement. Curiosity covered her face, but her eyes lit up with amazement. She could imagine all sorts of applications for rocks that lit up without needing to use electricity or a battery to power them.

Knowing she didn't have much time, Natalie reluctantly moved away from the wondrous sight and on to the next case. Her mouth turned down in disgust at the crimson colored creature. The think looked like a cross between a lobster and an extremely large centipede. As she looked at the thing, its' claws snapped at the glass while it moved forward and then backward in the case on hundreds of tiny legs. Natalie could see a slimy trail under the thing as it moved around the cage, darting toward the glass where Natalie stood every few seconds and clamping the claws open and shut. Natalie could see the rough edges lining the inside the claws, like the teeth of a saw blade. She was grateful the strange thing was trapped inside the case. If those claws got hold of a person's arm or leg they could cause considerable damage.

Natalie felt a shudder of repulsion combined with fear run through her and gladly turned away from the creature.

She moved past an empty case and over to the next one in line. She stopped and stared in horror at the thing that floated in the water filled case. At first, the tiny creature to her looked like an embryo of some kind. Then she frowned, realizing there was no way the thing could be human. She leaned forward slightly to get a better look. When she did, the thing bobbed in the water and turned slightly. As it did, three eyes in a monkey like face looked out at her.

Natalie's hand covered her mouth to hold in the scream that had started to rise up. Seeing the blank eyes, she realized the ghastly creature was dead. As she stared with revulsion, a large worm like insect crawled out of the thing's ear, leaving a trail of red slime behind it.

Natalie felt herself begin to gag and was afraid she was going to throw up. Pushing her hand tighter against her mouth, Natalie turned away from the horrendous sight and headed for the door.

On her way out, Natalie saw bottles of pills lining a shelf by the door that she hadn't seen on her way in. As her stomach began to do flip flops, Natalie decided she didn't need a sample bad enough to stop and she could worry about what the pills contained at another time.

She ran up the stairs, not bothering to even try to be quiet. Right now, the thought of someone finding her was the last thing on her mind. All she wanted at that moment was to get out of the hospital.

At the top of the stairs, she turned to the hallway and ran down it and to the doors that led outside.

As soon as she stepped out into the darkness, Natalie moved from the sidewalk to the grass, where she dropped on her knees and let all the contents of her stomach spill out onto the grass. When nothing was left, Natalie wiped a trembling hand across her mouth. She sat like that for a long time, trying to gulp in the clean, fresh air. Finally she stood on weakened legs and made her way to the apartment complex and then into her own apartment.

Going to the kitchen sink, Natalie turned on the faucet and using her hands scooped the water into her mouth over and over.

When she finished, she splashed the cool water on her face. Feeling faint, she turned off the water and made her way to a chair at the table. As she did she remembered her camera and berated herself for not getting pictures.

Natalie folded her arms and placing them on the table in front of her, she laid her head down and cried.

Chapter 11

After a night of tossing, turning and very little sleep, Natalie turned to look at the digital clock next to her bed. Watching the numbers slowly change, she finally decided she wouldn't be able to get any sleep and got up to put on a pot of coffee.

While it perked, Natalie went in to take a shower. Scrubbing herself until she was red as a beet, Natalie still couldn't wash away the dirty feeling that clung to her. The image of that thing floating in the glass case could never be washed from her mind.

After the shower and dressing, Natalie returned to the kitchen and with her mug of coffee in hand, stood and stared out the window as she waited for the white hospital van and Tony with it, to return.

She was just finishing the third cup of coffee when she finally saw the van drive in. Stepping closer to the window, Natalie stared, almost afraid to breathe, until she saw Tony step out.

She frowned, only seeing three patients emerge from the vehicle, and watched, dread building, as they were escorted into the structure by the two doctors.

The cup she was holding slipped from her fingers and crashed to the floor. The sound of the mug breaking was overly loud in the otherwise quiet of the room. Natalie barely heard it and didn't turn to clean up the mess until the hospital doors closed sealing the patients, now without Steve in their midst, inside the building.

As Natalie threw the pieces of the broken mug she'd finally picked up in the garbage she glanced out the window once more and saw Rita heading to work. Natalie sighed as she realized that meant she had eight long hours to kill until her shift started.

Without much to fill her time, Natalie went through and scrubbed her apartment, even though it wasn't dirty. Then she tried reading a novel. After the first few pages, she realized she hadn't remembered one word she'd read and put the book back on the shelf. By then, it was noon, but Natalie knew she wasn't going to be able to eat. Instead she found a notebook and began writing down everything she knew about the two doctors running the psychiatric hospital. As she wrote what she'd seen in the basement, first she felt nauseous, it didn't take long for her anger to override her initial emotion. After writing everything down, Natalie folded the several sheets of paper and put them in her pocket. She wanted Tony to read them. She felt she'd captured not only the incidents that had happened, but also her feelings about what was going on down in the written words better than she knew she could express them verbally.

She also hoped she'd get the chance to make copies of what she'd written down. She had no idea where or to whom she could send them, but she knew she needed to find a way for both her and Tony to get away from Whitmore Hills. When they did, she had to find a way to let others know what had been happening here at the hospital and also up in the cabin in the woods.

Natalie looked at her watch, two more hours and she could begin her shift. She still planned on leaving Tony for her last patient of the day. She only hoped she'd be able to keep her mind on her other patients while she was with them. Maybe she'd even get lucky and they'd have something to add, especially concerning the absence of Steve Lincoln.

By the time the two hours passed, Natalie was sure she'd walked at least five miles, nervously pacing a few feet at a time across the length of her apartment. As anxious as she was to get to the hospital, the minute she stepped out of her apartment, she felt like turning around, running back in and hiding from this whole mess.

Instead, she took a deep breath and walked determinedly to the hospital doors and then inside. Before heading upstairs, she ducked into the computer room and made three copies of each page she had written earlier. As the copies printed, she glanced at the doorway several times, expecting someone to come in and ask what she was up to. When no one did, Natalie folded the papers and slid them in her pocket, before hurrying up the stairway.

Going to Megan's room first, Natalie slid her card in the slot and stepped inside. Looking over at the hospital bed, Natalie frowned. Megan was curled into a ball facing away from the door. She didn't move when the door shut behind Natalie nor when Natalie called out her name.
Placing her clipboard on the table, she stared at Megan's back. Natalie's first thought was that when she stepped over, she'd discover the woman was dead.

Shaking the morbid thought from her head, Natalie made her way to the bed. Reaching out, she touched Megan's arm and relief flooded through her at the warmth of the woman's skin. "Megan, It's just Natalie, are you feeling okay?"

She could barely hear Megan's mumbled reply. "Steve's gone."
Then she rolled over and stared at Natalie with blood shot eyes. "He's a patient here, or he was. I know he escaped, but I don't

even know what he looked like. How can that be possible?"

Natalie just stared at Megan a moment. Now she knew why Steve hadn't returned with the others, or at least she knew the story that was going to be used.
Reaching out, Natalie lightly touched Megan's arm. "I'm not sure what's happening, but you need to settle down. You'll make yourself sick getting all worked up. I think I'd better check your blood pressure. Just let me go and get my equipment."

Megan was shaking her head. "That's just what Rita said earlier, but I can't help it."

Natalie tried to give Megan what she hoped was a reassuring smile. "I'll get my things and then we can talk about it."

Going in the bathroom, Natalie unlocked the closet and pulled out the things she needed. By the time she returned to the main room, Megan was sitting up on her bed. She sat still while Natalie checked her and then as she took the time to put her equipment away.

Stepping in the room again, Natalie grabbed a chair and brought it over next to Megan's bed. "Why don't you tell me what you remember? Try not to get upset though. Your blood pressure is borderline as it is. If it gets higher, I'll have to call in one of the doctors."

Megan's eyes grew wide as she ran a hand through her dark hair and shook her head. "I don't think I want to see either of the doctors right now."

Megan took in a couple of deep breaths and Natalie nodded. "That's better, why don't we start with your trip. Tell me about that."

A crease appeared across Megan's forehead as she tried to remember. "I enjoyed the stay at the cabin. The fire was mesmerizing. It was nice to rest and get out of the hospital."

Now it was Natalie's eyes that grew wide and then narrowed as she stared at Megan, not liking the robotic quality of the woman's voice. "Tell me what happened to Steve."

Megan shook her head, her eyes sad. "Poor Steve, he was delusional and acting crazy. The doctors tried to help him, but Steve ran off into the woods."
Megan sighed. "It was an unfortunate incident. I'm just glad I'm safe here at the hospital and getting such good care."

Natalie stared at Megan. "Is that all you remember? Did you talk to the other patients, or even the doctors?'

Looking at Natalie, the dark eyes now looked frightened. "I don't know, I can't remember anything else. I don't even know how many patients were on the trip. I only know of one and he ran off in the woods."
Shaking her head, Megan started to cry.

Slipping a hand around Megan's shoulder, Natalie tried to find some way to comfort the distraught woman. "It's okay Megan, the stress of the event could be what's causing your lack of recall. Our mind does funny things to compensate for events that are devastating and hard for us to comprehend. Your mind is blocking the memories that would be hurtful to you."

Megan wiped the tears from her eyes and stared at Natalie. "That's what Rita said. Do you really believe that's what's going on?"

Even though she didn't believe what she was telling Megan at all, Natalie nodded. "I'm sure that's what is happening. I think the best thing you can do right now is just try and get yourself some rest. Everything's going to be okay, and like you said, you're safe here in the hospital."

As she nodded, Megan stretched out in her bed. "Thanks Natalie, I already feel better."

Natalie smiled. "I'm glad to hear that. You go ahead and get that rest. I'm just going to do a little cleaning before I leave."

Placing a hand on Megan's arm, Natalie gently rubbed it. "Everything is going to be just fine."

As she said the words, Natalie hated lying to her patient. She also didn't know what else she could do.

By the time she cleaned the bathroom and straightened the rest of the small area, Natalie was pleased to see Megan had taken her advice and had gone to sleep.

Leaving the room, Natalie stood out in the hallway for a long while, collecting herself, before she felt ready to head for Ted's room. Stepping in the door, she found him sitting at the table.

A big smile appeared on his face. "Well, hello, nice of you to drop by."

Staring at Ted, Natalie knew he had no idea who she was. That was normal for Ted and also meant that his dementia and almost nonexistent memory wouldn't be much help to her.

That was also why Ted's next words took Natalie by surprise. "Have they found Steve yet?"

Trying to hide her astonishment at his question, Natalie pulled out a chair and sat down opposite from the man. Placing her clipboard on the table, she shook her head. "I'm afraid no one has heard anything yet."

With a sigh, Ted nodded. "They probably never will. I hate to say it, but I think Steve's lost in those woods."
Ted shuddered. "The forest is scary."

Glad for his last statement and an opening for the questions she wanted to ask, Natalie nodded. "The woods can be frightening, but you felt safe in the cabin didn't you?"

The round face bobbed up and down enthusiastically, enhancing Ted's double chin. "Oh yes, the cabin is wonderful. I always enjoy my stay there and the chance to get out of the hospital. I'm glad to be back here now though and safe in my room. It was such an unfortunate incident that Steve ran off into the woods like that."

Now, Natalie knew she couldn't hide the shocked look on her face. Luckily Ted didn't seem to notice her reaction to his words, so similar to those she'd just heard from Megan. Natalie stood. "I better get my things and check your vitals before we get talking and I forget."

A look of confusion covered Ted's face, but he nodded and watched Natalie walk away. As she entered the bathroom, Natalie stepped to the closet and unlocked it with shaking hands so she could retrieve her supplies. She took her time, trying to soothe her uneasiness before returning to the table where Ted still sat.

After recording Ted's vitals, Natalie realized she'd been so shaken up in Megan's room she hadn't recorded anything in her first patient's chart. Nor had she asked any of the questions that had been given for the day. Natalie sighed, knowing that she'd just have to make something up. She looked at the questions the doctors had written down for Ted, then flipped the pages to see almost duplicate ones for Megan and also for Tony. She could easily see the theme of the questioning and had a dreadful feeling that she knew why the doctors had put those specific questions on the charts today. They were trying to make sure the patients didn't remember the time in the cabin as it really happened.

Looking at the clipboard she read the first of the three questions. "How do you feel about Steve running off like that?"

Ted shook his head, the usually happy eyes now sad. "I think it was an awful thing to do. The people here at the hospital take good care of us. That's no way to repay them."

Nodding, Natalie smiled. "I'm glad to hear you think you are receiving good care." Natalie looked at the second question and didn't bother asking it. If she asked how Ted felt the trip went, she knew she'd get the same robotic answer about it being relaxing and enjoyable. Instead, she moved to the last one on the list. "Do you feel Doctor Sullivan and Doctor Harrell handled the situation correctly?"

Ted nodded. "They did all they could. Their efforts to stop Steve were nothing short of valiant. It was just such an unfortunate incident."

Natalie felt her heart skip a beat, hearing those words, unfortunate incident, yet again. She was positive now all the patients had been given the same hypnotic suggestions before they returned from the cabin. She felt Ted staring at her and turned to him and smiled. "Thanks Ted, you did great today. I'm just going to go ahead and straighten up your room if you don't mind. Then I think it should be almost time for your dinner."

Laughing, Ted rubbed his stomach. "Great, I'm starving."

Natalie quickly straightened Ted's room and then locked the equipment she'd used back in the closet before telling Ted to have a great night and leaving the room.

From there, Natalie made her way down to the cafeteria. She wasn't hungry, but she knew the guards always served the patients their dinner during her own break. Grabbing a cup of coffee, Natalie found a table in the empty room and sat down, grateful right now no one was around. She took a few minutes to fill out the charts on her clipboard. This was the first time she could remember since she had started working at Whitmore Hills that the questions given the patients were virtually identical. Her mind felt like it was stuck in a whirlwind as she tried to imagine what might have really happened up at Doctor Sullivan's cabin. She knew now that Tony's theory was dead on. The two doctors that ran the psychiatric hospital were hypnotizing their patients. She also had to go with the assumption the two were also sending those same patients to the other worlds through the tears Tony had told her about. The little bit of conversation she'd been lucky enough to overhear at her stakeout of the cabin confirmed Tony's theories and her worst fears.

Natalie sighed as she stood and stepped over to the large coffee pot the cafeteria staff always kept filled. By the time she sat back down and finished her drink, the time had come for Natalie to see her last and most important patient of her shift.
Throwing away her Styrofoam cup, Natalie

grabbed her clipboard and headed upstairs for Tony's room.

As she reached Tony's locked door, Natalie hesitated just a brief second before sliding her card in and pushing the door inward.

Sitting at the table, Tony stood and smiled, relieved to see the woman he had grown to love in the short time he'd know her.
He'd been afraid after telling her his crazy story and then asking her to go to the cabin to find a way to verify it, that Natalie might not show up today.
Stepping over, Tony pulled Natalie into a hug. She looked up at the camera and hoped no one was watching. She pointed at the table. "Sit down Tony. Before we start, I need to remind you that the camera up there on the ceiling is on twenty four seven. There's no audio feed so at least we don't have to worry about anything we say being recorded."

Tony nodded as he sat down. "I knew they kept the camera running. I hope you're not in trouble."

Natalie shook her head. "One of the guards, Vann Shields, was good enough to scramble the video of us kissing. I think he's someone we can trust. Before we start, I'm going in the bathroom, thankfully no cameras are set up in there. I've written down everything I know about what's been happening at the hospital and at the cabin. You need to read it and keep that copy hidden somewhere safe. I have one for me and two more I need to find a place to mail them to. I'll grab my equipment while I'm in there and we'll act like this is just a normal visit."

Natalie waited for Tony to nod, then she went into the bathroom. She returned a few minutes later and began working on getting Tony's vital statistics. As she took his blood pressure, she stared into the green eyes she found so fascinating. "Before we talk about what I found out, I want you to tell me what you think happened up at the cabin."

Frowning, Tony shrugged and drew in a breath. "The same as always I guess, other than the fact one of the patients ran off into the woods. His name was Steve. It was really an unfortunate incident."

Natalie couldn't stop the gasp that escaped. Tony frowned at her. "What's wrong?"

Natalie shook her head. "I'll explain in a minute. What else went on up there?"

Still frowning, Tony continued. "It was peaceful, just sitting and watching the fire was so relaxing. It was good to rest and be away from the hospital, even for just a short while."

Natalie nodded. "What did the doctors do or say about what Steve did?"

Tony shook his head. "They were upset of course. They did make a valiant effort to stop him though."

At those words, Natalie's mouth dropped open and she stared at Tony. "What was this valiant effort the two doctors made?"

Tony frowned then. "I'm not sure, but they did all they could. Steve's gone and I don't think they'll find him."

Natalie frowned at that statement. "Why don't you think they'll find him?"

Tony shrugged. "That's just how I feel. What's going on Natalie? What really happened up there? Did you do like we planned?"

Natalie nodded. "I drove up as close as I felt safe doing and then I hiked in the rest of the way to the cabin. I crouched behind a bush below a window and heard the doctors talking, mostly Doctor Sullivan. He talked about giving all you patient's drugs, then he hypnotized all of you and planned on sending you out through a doorway to another world to get samples. Doctor Sullivan and Doctor Harrell are using what you bring back to make new drugs with. I don't know what happened to Steve, but I'm fairly certain he's dead."

Natalie shook her head. "I came back here after that and went down to the lab in the basement. They have a lot of strange things down there. Including some kind of bizarre almost human creature floating dead in a glass case."

A shiver ran through Natalie. "The thing had three eyes."

Staring at Tony, Natalie could see what she was saying didn't surprise him. "Have you seen something like that before?"

With a sigh, Tony nodded. "I've seen a lot of weird things in the other worlds. I've also seen some amazing and wondrous sights and places you wouldn't believe. If the other patients could remember the worlds, they'd tell you the same thing."

Natalie shrugged. "I think they already might have done that. The other patients have told me about dreams they've had and feelings they get. Some are horrific nightmares and others are almost like heaven. In fact, Steve was talking about wanting to paint a picture that was what might easily be mistaken for heaven." Natalie felt like crying knowing in her heart Steve was dead and would never get the chance to put that place on canvas. "What are we going to do Tony? We can't let them get away with this."

Tony stared at Natalie and then shook his head. "No one would ever believe this story and the doctors are going to make sure I don't get out to tell it."

With a sigh, Natalie's head of dark blonde hair dropped and she rubbed her face. "We have to do something. What those two have down in the lab has to be enough to put them in jail."

Tony shook his head. "I don't think so. They could say those things were just something they fabricated for experimentation. You could never prove where they actually came from. Don't forget, I'm a patient here and diagnosed as delusion and maybe even a few other psychiatric terms. No one is going to believe I can not only see the tears between worlds, but step into them."

As she thought about that, Natalie frowned. "Then we have to find a way to stop them on our own. Look what they've done to you and the other patients. I'm even beginning to wonder about Shelley Morris. I don't think she just walked off the job now. I think she got too inquisitive and the doctors made her vanish."

Staring at Natalie, Tony's green eyes darkened. "That's exactly why you shouldn't get involved. I know we haven't known each other long, but I love you Natalie, I don't want anything to happen to you. The best thing for you to do is walk away from all of this. Go somewhere that the doctors can't find you and forget you ever heard of me or Whitmore Hills."

The brown eyes looking at Tony, sparkled with emotion. "I love you too Tony, and that's why I can't walk away. We need to end the doctor's plans and find a way to shut down this hospital. That's the only way I could live with myself. If I left here, I couldn't stand the way I feel. I would be a failure to you and to the other patients. We can figure this out Tony, we have to."

Ignoring the cameras, Tony stood and stepped over to Natalie and pulled her in a hug. "Then that's what we'll do."

Chapter 12

For almost a month since Natalie and Tony
had decided they needed to figure a way to
shut down the hospital and stop the doctors,
the two had used every one of Natalie's
visits to come up with a plan.

Natalie felt the two of them could trust Vann
and with Tony's approval, filled him in on
what she knew about what was happening at
the hospital and the cabin before asking for
his help. Not only was Vann open to the
plan, but truly believed the extraordinary
story Natalie shared with him. At the same
time, Vann told Natalie he'd heard of others
like Tony who could see the abnormal
openings that sat between worlds. Vann also
felt he had two places that would be perfect
for Natalie to send her letters when the time
was right. One on the east coast and one on
the opposite end of the United States on the
west coast. Both were extremely liberal

publications that Vann assured Natalie wouldn't just dismiss her letters as coming from a psychotic individual. Especially when they saw the two doctors names included in the story. According to Vann, a few years back, Doctor Sullivan and Doctor Harrell had been accused of some unscrupulous acts. The lawyers, the doctors had paid incredulous amounts of money to, had gotten the charges dropped and the scandal hushed.

Natalie acted as a kind of mediator between Tony and Vann. Neither of the men felt Vann should be going to Tony's room unless it was to deliver a meal and that usually wasn't part of his job because of the overnight shift he worked.

Natalie had first approached Vann a week after the episode at the cabin. In the two weeks since then, the trio had been busy scheming and planning for a way to not only take down the doctors, but to shut down Whitmore Hills. They had decided the best time to do anything would have to be during the next planned trip for the patients to

Doctor Sullivan's cabin and now that was just over a week away.

Today, Natalie was in the computer room and had just finished putting in the stats from her visits into the patients' files on the computer.

Vann was laughing. "I don't know why you bother writing all that crap down. You could just skip it and type in whatever you wanted into those files. I could think of a lot of information you could add that would freak a couple of doctors out."

Natalie shook her head. "No thanks, right now, the last thing I want to do is have either of the doctors suspicious or upset. I don't want anything to jeopardize our plans."

With a shrug, Vann nodded. "I guess you're right, the plan we're working on is risky enough without any snags."
Vann frowned. "Is Tony doing okay? I've been watching him on the camera and he doesn't look like he's sleeping too well. It seems like every time I look up at the screen

the other two patients are sound asleep, but Tony is always either sitting up in his bed or pacing the floor."

Natalie sighed. "I don't know, I think he's more worried about my getting hurt than anything else."

Vann smiled. "It's nice to have someone care about you that much. I'm glad you and Tony were able to find each other."

A smile lit up Natalie's eyes as she thought about Tony, then she frowned.
"Too bad it was under these circumstances. Almost two months ago, I was so ecstatic to be hired on here. I needed a job badly and getting this one was like a dream come true. I guess there really is a slim line between dreams and nightmares. I wouldn't have met Tony or you and that would have been a tremendous loss. On the nightmare side, I did meet two doctors who are a lot more psychotic that any of the patients they are supposed to be helping."

Vann laughed, the blue eyes full of mischief. "At least you can't complain your life is boring, and I think the fun and games have only just begun."

Seeing the worried look on Natalie's face, Vann smiled. "Hey, we've got this. In my book, the good guys always win, right?"

With a sigh, Natalie couldn't help but smile at Vann's enthusiasm. "I guess believing in something is half the battle."

Then Natalie nodded. "So yeah, we got this."

Natalie stood. "I better head out. Rusty's on the overnight shift. He's so nice, it's hard for me not to share what's going to happen around here in a week."

The grin Vann gave Natalie could soften the hardest of hearts. "I'm not going to let any of the nurses or guards get hurt. Remember they were misled into believing that the doctors were here to help the patients too. They're victims as much as the patients are. Natalie, we've been working on this plan two weeks. If I didn't think it was one we could pull off, believe me, I'd be the first to say so. Now, go get some rest."

Natalie smiled. "Thanks Vann, I hate that I asked you to be part of this, but I'm damn glad you agreed to help and I'm proud to call you my friend."

Vann slid an arm around Natalie's shoulders. "That feeling is mutual. You can tell Tony I feel the same way towards him on your next visit to his room too."

Natalie smiled. "I'll do that, good night Vann."

Leaving the hospital, Natalie headed for her apartment, glad she'd left early enough that she didn't run into Rusty on her way. Entering her apartment, the first thing Natalie did, like she had after every shift in the last week, was head in to her bedroom and go to the closet.
Pulling out a dark blue backpack, she checked the contents, yet again. Inside she'd placed two changes of clothes, all the money she'd retrieved from her bank account and the two envelopes, addressed and stamped. They contained the pages she'd written about all that had happened.
After every shift, she checked the pack,

always terrified someone would have by some means learned about what she, Tony and Vann were planning. Scared the bag would be empty and that either Doctor Sullivan or Doctor Harrell would be banging on her door to take her away from the hospital and worse, from Tony.
Reassuring herself the bag had gone untouched. Natalie felt like crying with relief.

As Natalie got undressed and slipped into her nightgown, she laid down on top of her bed. The weather had gotten warm enough that there was no use for covers.

Natalie stared up at the ceiling, hoping not only for sleep, but that the next week and a half would pass quickly.

Chapter 13

The time passed with excruciating slowness. Finally though, Natalie found herself in Tony's room the night before the scheduled trip to the cabin. The doctors would be taking over the patient's care in the morning and headed to the cabin shortly before their evening meal, giving the employees all the extra monthly day off.

Natalie was placing the ear plugs she had obtained on Tony's bathroom sink beside the other object she had left for him. That way Tony could find the items away from the prying eyes of the room's security camera. The plugs were special. They were tiny enough they could be placed far enough into the wearer's ear that they were virtually invisible. A string, smaller than a single strand of human hair was connected to the plugs, allowing a person a way to remove the devices.

Or, at least that was Natalie's hope. The last

thing Tony needed was one of the doctors to spot the plugs before or during Doctor Sullivan's hypnosis of the patients.

With a final look at the sink bench, Natalie stepped out of the bathroom holding her blood pressure machine and stethoscope. She looked over at Tony standing in the room. "Why don't we get those vitals Tony?"

Moving to sit on his bed, Tony nodded, but he looked at Natalie with curiosity filled green eyes. She smiled. "I put the ear plugs on the sink bench. I don't think you'll have any problems using them. Just remember, once you put them in, you won't be able to hear anything. I hope you're a good actor. You'll have to not only pretend you can hear the doctors talking to you, but that you're being hypnotized."

With a shrug, Tony smiled. "I've never tried acting, although I have been accused of it. Mostly by my parents. They thought my explanations of the other worlds were nothing more than big lies and that I was a wonderful actor as I recalled what I saw. I think they thought that I told the stories to get attention. Don't worry, I'll be fine. What about Vann? Is he still doing okay with all of this?"

With an animated nod, Natalie laughed. "To tell you the truth, I think he's actually looking forward to the whole thing. He's looking at the plan as some kind of great adventure."

Tony laughed. "I guess in a way that's exactly what it is. I'm just glad he believes all you've told him. Not many people are that accepting, especially with the nature of the stories."

Natalie nodded. "I just hope the two places he suggested that I send my letters to, end up being as open minded as Vann is." Natalie's face turned serious. "Remember, don't eat or drink anything tomorrow that either Doctor Sullivan or Doctor Harrell bring to you. I don't know how they administered the drugs to help control the patients, but from what I overheard at the cabin, you were all definitely drugged. The doctors are going to have all day to find a way to get those medications into you. I talked to Vann and he's going to find a way to slip in and bring you some extra snacks later, before the doctors take charge of your treatment."

Tony smiled. "I'll be fine, if I have to go a day without food. I won't starve. That's the least of our worries. What about the other thing we talked about, were you able to get that for me?"

Natalie didn't have to ask what Tony was asking about. "I left it in the bathroom. Are you sure the doctors didn't check you before they put you in the van and escorted all of you from the hospital?"

Shrugging, Tony shook his head. "I can definitely remember the doctors checking our pockets when we were preparing to get in the van to come back here, but I don't think they were worried about any of us taking something from here to the cabin."

Still worried about the idea, Natalie's nod was given reluctantly.
"Just find a good hiding place."

She stared at Tony. "I don't know about you, but I'm scared to death."

A reassuring and compassionate smile covered Tony's face. "Everything is going to be fine Natalie, I just know it."
Tony pointed at the blood pressure monitor Natalie still held. "Why don't I help you put that away?"

Standing, Natalie headed for the bathroom with Tony right behind her. After locking up the equipment, Natalie and Tony moved to the corner of the bathroom where no cameras could record them.

Pulling Natalie into a hug, Tony held her tight for a moment and then pulling back slightly, he leaned down to kiss her. Beginning slowly, the kiss intensified and both felt the hunger for each other grow. Natalie pulled back first, out of breath. "I can't wait until we can find out just where that is going to lead."

Tony smiled. "It won't be too long. By tomorrow night, our plan will be accomplished and we can explore that and our relationship together."

After one more, less passionate kiss, Natalie stepped from the bathroom and the two walked into Tony's room. Although reluctant to leave, Natalie knew she had to go. Neither of them wanted to do anything to make others think there was anything different about tonight's visit.

Heading downstairs to the computer room, Natalie stepped in, surprised to see Rex Corgin seated and looking up at the monitors. "Hi Rex, you're here kind of late aren't you?"

Turning back, Rex's attention went from the monitors to look at Natalie, as he nodded. "Vann's running late, I told him I'd cover for him. Of course, that means he owes me big time. I'll have to find something really good to get even."

Natalie laughed. "Now, why doesn't that surprise me?"
She held up her clipboard. "Would I be

bothering you if I take a minute and add some things to the patient's files?"

Rex shook his head. "Not at all, in fact. I think I'll run to the cafeteria while you're here and grab myself a drink."
Rex stood. "Will you keep an eye on the monitors for me?"

Looking up at the screens, Natalie nodded. "No problem, it doesn't look like there's much to watch though."

Rex shrugged. "There hardly ever is. The job's boring as hell, but you can't beat the pay. I'll be right back."

By the time Rex had returned. Natalie had finished recording her statistics for the day.

She left the hospital and headed for her apartment and what she knew was going to be a sleepless night.

Chapter 14

Standing in her apartment the next morning, Natalie kept glancing out her kitchen window even though she knew the white hospital van wasn't scheduled to leave until around four o'clock.

Natalie walked back through her apartment. She had a box she was slowly filling up with things she couldn't leave behind, mostly mementos she had from her parents. She wasn't sure what Tony would think about the extra baggage, but she couldn't leave those things behind.

When she finished, Natalie carried the box and her backpack out and locked them in the trunk of her car. She'd already prepared a speech in case anyone caught her. She was going to tell them shed found some junk she didn't need and the next time they made a trip to town she was planning on taking the stuff to a second hand store.

With that taken care of, Natalie went back to her apartment. Looking up at the clock and seeing it was only eleven a.m. she sighed. Four o'clock was taking its sweet time getting here. She thought about trying to eat something when she heard a knock on the door. With a frown on her face, Natalie walked to the door and opened it to find Rita standing there. "Come on in, what are you doing up? I figured you'd take the chance and sleep in until well past noon."

As she stepped in, Rita laughed. "Sleeping in until eleven was enough. What about you? You're used to sleeping in. Your normal shift doesn't even start until four."

Natalie nodded. "I couldn't sleep so decided just to get up and sort through some of my stuff. When I moved, I just threw everything I owned in boxes, glad to be out of my old place. I found a few things I didn't need and already boxed them up and put them in my car. They can stay there until I have a chance to take them somewhere. Can I get you something to drink?"

Rita smiled. "Maybe just a glass of water for now. When we head to the rec room at the hospital I can start in on the wine."

With a nod, Natalie went to the fridge and got Rita a bottle of water and then the two sat down on the couch and spent an hour or two visiting. Rita looked at her watch and her dark brown eyes opened wide. "Wow, I can't believe that it's three o'clock already. I better get back to my place and get ready. I'll stop by here when I'm done and we can head over to the hospital together."

Natalie smiled. "Sounds like a plan. I need to get changed myself."

As soon as Rita left, Natalie looked out her kitchen window and stared at the van, parked beside the hospital, hoping she would see the patient's being loaded. Her shoulders dropped when she didn't see anyone yet.
Dropping the curtain she'd been peeking out of, Natalie turned and headed for her bedroom and stood in front of her closet. She wasn't sure what she should be wearing and decided on the white shirt she had

previously decided to wear because of what her and Vann had set up and also a pair of jeans. She slipped on her best tennis shoes and then went in the kitchen to sit at the table and wait.

An hour later as she looked out the window for the millionth time, her heart skipped a beat and then took off on a full gallop. The doctors were loading the three patients into the van. Tony was the first to climb in the van and Natalie hoped that meant he hadn't been drugged and that the doctors hadn't found the things Tony was hiding.
As the van pulled away, Natalie heard the knock on her door. As she opened it, she was surprised to see not just Rita, but Carl and Rusty standing there. Rita smiled. "I found these two bums just hanging around and thought they might be fun at a party. What do you think?"

Stepping out to join them, Natalie laughed. "I guess they'll have to do. I think they're both kinda cute."

Rusty smiled and ran a hand through his brownish red hair. "You two don't know how lucky you are. I'm a great dancer and Carl has those surfer boy good looks, how could you go wrong?"

Both Natalie and Rita rolled their eyes and started laughing. Rita slipped an arm through Rusty's. "Just as long as you buy me a glass of wine, I'm okay with that."

Natalie took Carl's arm and the four walked together to the hospital. Going in, they went straight to the recreation room where Arthur, Rex and Vann were already sitting.
Vann stood. "Glad everyone's here. I ordered pizza. They should be showing up with the delivery in a few minutes. There's cold beer and wine in the fridge. Arthur also grabbed a bottle of vodka if anyone wants to try that."

Natalie smiled. "I'll just take wine. What do you think goes the best with pizza, red or white?"

Vann laughed. "I'd say red, definitely red."

Everyone got their drinks and then sat down and visited until the pizza delivery man knocked on the front door of the hospital. Vann and Arthur went out and then came back carrying four boxes of pizza that they placed on the table.

Natalie and Vann sat next to each other at the table and the others took places around the large table. Everyone was joking and laughing. Looking at his watch, Vann turned to stare at Natalie, who gave him an almost indiscernible nod. He stood up and as he did, he bumped Natalie's hand holding her glass of wine. The red stain quickly spread on her white blouse. Natalie stood brushing herself off. Rita stood next to her. "Let me go find a washrag or something. That is going to be a pain to get out Natalie."

Shaking her head, Natalie tried to smile. "It'll be okay, this isn't that great of a shirt anyway. I think I better run back to my apartment and find a dry shirt though."

Rita nodded. "Do you want me to come with you?"

Natalie shook her head. "No, you stay here and finish your dinner. I'll just be gone a minute."

Vann was shaking his head. "I'm really sorry Natalie. If it's ruined, I'll gladly pay for a new one."

Natalie smiled at him, trying not to laugh at the planned accident he was apologizing for. "Don't even worry about it, just hold down the fort while I'm gone and when I come back you can wait on me and bring me wine all night."

Nodding, Vann smiled. "It's a deal."

Natalie hurried out of the hospital and headed for her apartment. She couldn't believe how well that had worked. As she went inside, she changed her shirt, for scrubs with front pockets and then went back to the kitchen and looked out the window, waiting for the next signal from Vann that would allow her to drive out of here and to the cabin without being seen.

After Natalie left the hospital, Vann looked at the others. "I feel awful about that."

Standing at the fridge now, Rita was refilling her own wine glass, she turned to Vann. "I wouldn't worry about it. Natalie is making good money, she can always buy a new shirt. Why don't we get a game of pool going while we wait for her to get back?"

Vann frowned. "You go ahead, I need to go grab something from the computer room. I'll be right back."

As Vann left the room the others went over to the pool table and split up into teams and began playing pool.

None of them noticed that Vann didn't head for the computer office. Instead he went to the front desk of the hospital and pulled out the item he had hid there the night before. He took the smoke bomb and walked over to the stairs that led to the hospital's basement. Lighting the bomb, he threw it down the stairs and waited a few moments until he could see the smoke beginning to drift into the stairwell, then he walked over and pulled the fire alarm that sat on the wall.

The sound of the alarm was loud enough that Natalie heard it from her apartment and whispered a silent thank you to Vann for the idea. As Natalie went out and started her car, Vann was stepping back into the rec room and was ordering the others to head for the front doors of the hospital.

"I don't know if we have a real fire or not but head outside and get across the street. I think the fire started down in the lab and I have no idea what the doctors have stashed down there. Hopefully it isn't something that will blow. We're safer across the road until the fire department gets here, they're hooked up to our system."

Once outside, Vann moved to the side of the others so he could watch for Natalie leaving in her car. As soon as he saw her, he pushed the button on the device in his pocket and the explosions began.

Natalie had a hard time ignoring the sound behind her. She had faith in Vann and knew he wouldn't set off the bombs he had placed in the basement lab until he knew everyone was out of the hospital and safe.

Natalie stepped on the gas and drove as quickly as she dared toward the cabin in the woods. About half way to her destination, Natalie could no longer hear the sound of the alarm or the fire engines she knew would be headed to the hospital. She gave a silent thanks for that. The last thing she wanted was for either Doctor Sullivan or Doctor Harrell to hear and recognize the noise for what it was.

Natalie parked her car not far from the place she had used before on her last clandestine trip to the cabin. Getting out she hurried to the cabin and stood next to the window so she could hear what was happening inside. The sound of Doctor Sullivan's voice made Natalie's muscle tense and the hair on her body stand on end.

"That's right, just focus on the fire."

Without thinking she ran for the front door and then flinging open the thankfully unlocked door, Natalie rushed inside. Pulling the hypodermic needle from the pocket of her scrubs, Natalie ran over to where Doctor Harrell was standing watching Doctor Sullivan address the patients. Lifting her arm, Natalie plunged the needle into Doctor Harrell's neck just as he turned at the sound of the door opening. The dark blue eyes opened wide as the doctor reached up to claw at the needle sticking out of his neck. Before he could pull it out he dropped to his knees.

Ignoring him, Natalie turned to look over at Tony who used the advantage of surprise to pull the ear plugs from his ears and then stand and run toward Doctor Sullivan. The doctor, whose attention had been focused on Natalie and Doctor Harrell, turned as Tony ran into him. The motion knocked him to the floor then Tony stabbed the doctor with the needle Natalie had left for him back at the hospital bathroom. Running over, Natalie helped Tony to his feet and then pulled him into a hug. Together the two walked over to where Ted and Megan still sat on the chairs, oblivious to the commotion in the room.

Tony took a deep breath and looked at the

blank faces. "The fire is out. It's time to head back."

As the two looked up at him, Tony turned to Ted. "I need you to get Megan in the van and drive her back to the hospital. Vann will be waiting for the two of you and will help you. Just go and find Vann. Can you do that?"

Ted nodded. "I can do that, what about the doctors. Shouldn't they be coming with us?"

Tony couldn't stop the laugh that seemed to fill the air. "The doctors are going to stay here and rest for a while. You two need to go ahead and get back to the hospital."

Natalie and Tony helped Ted and Megan out to the van and then waited for them to leave before they headed back inside the cabin where both doctors were laying on the floor in a drug induced sleep.
Looking at Natalie, Tony frowned. "We need to find something to tie them up. I don't want them getting away."

The two went out to the kitchen where they found some rope and bungee cords. Heading back to the living room they roughly pulled the doctors across the floor and into the kitchen where they tied them up and then fastened both of them to the water pipes by the sink. When they were done Tony looked down at the men, hatred darkening the green eyes.

Seeing the look, Natalie took a hold of Tony's arm. "Don't do anything Tony. These two will get what's coming to them. Vann will see to that. We just need to get out of here."

Reluctantly, Tony nodded. What he really felt like doing was beating both men until they were unrecognizable. He knew Natalie was right and turned away from the men, "Where did you leave your car?"

Natalie pointed toward the woods. "It's just back that way."

Tony nodded. "Let's go, I need you to do some driving. I was able to spit out the pills they gave me, but I'm still feeling a little drowsy."

A frown crossed Natalie's forehead. "Where are we going? I thought we'd head to town and then into one of those rips between worlds, that's what we talked about."

Tony nodded. "I don't like where the ones around here lead, but I know one we can use. We need to head back toward Portsmouth. There's a place behind my parent's house I went to when I was a teenager. I never forgot it and always wanted to go back. I think you'll like it."

Natalie only nodded, her future was in Tony's hands now. The couple walked back to Natalie's car with their arms wrapped around each other's waists.

When they got there, Natalie got in the driver's seat and Tony crawled into the passenger side.

Before they left, Natalie got back out of the car, remembering something she needed to do. Stepping around to the trunk, she opened it and pulled her two special letters from her backpack.

Getting back in the car, Natalie followed Tony's directions and drove quickly using back roads that took them around the smoke they could see coming from the direction of the hospital. They could hear the sounds of sirens and both hoped they included fire and police ready to investigate what was happening at Whitmore Hills.

On their way through Portsmouth, Natalie took the time to drive to the back of the local post office and dropped her letters in the large metal mailboxes that sat there. As she did, she said a silent prayer that the receivers would be like Vann and believe the words that had been written on the enclosed sheets of paper.

An hour later the two sat in the car and Natalie stared in astonishment at what looked like a castle to her. She pointed at the house. "That's where your parents live?"

Staring over at the house, Tony nodded. When he spoke his voice was bitter. "Most of the time. They also have a couple of vacation homes. Drive around the block. The place I want is on the other side of the house."

Putting the car in gear, Natalie drove around the house. It was dark outside, but she could still see fairly well on the end of June night. The back of the property was well hidden by large tees. Tony showed her where to park and then stared off to his left. Then he pointed. "It's right over there."

As they stepped out of the car, Natalie turned to Tony and pointed at the trunk of her car. "I have a backpack in there and a box of a few things I couldn't stand to leave behind."

Tony nodded. "That's fine, if you can take the backpack, I'll carry the box."

Opening the trunk, Natalie grabbed her backpack and slung it over her shoulder and then waited for Tony to get hold of the box before she closed the trunk and with a drawn in breath, she turned and followed toward the tear she hadn't seen until Tony started to step through and then turned back to smile at her. "I'd take your hand or even carry you over the threshold but my arms are full at the moment."

Natalie laughed. "I'll let you slide this time, but I still plan on holding you to that promise to carry me over the threshold."

As Natalie stepped over to Tony, she stared in amazement at the rip, he stood halfway through, looking now more like a doorway and to the small portion of landscape she could see on the other side of the opening. Natalie was reminded of the beautiful picture Steve had told her he wanted to paint. The memory of that day felt like it was ages old and Natalie felt her heart ache for the man she had no doubt was dead. A death that was a waste and an abomination. One that so far had gone unnoticed and unmarked by those who loved the man. She wanted to be able to change that someday.

Thinking about that, Natalie could only hope between Vann and the letters she had sent that the doctors would have to pay for what they did. Seeing the green eyes staring at her, Natalie smiled and followed Tony through the opening and into another world.

Chapter 15

In two newspaper offices, twenty four hundred miles apart, almost identical things were happening.

In one office, Renee Madison had been handed an envelope by her assistant.
"I hate to bother you, but I think you might want to have a look at this."
With those words, the assistant stepped out of the room, knowing Renee would want to be alone to read the contents of the letter.

Renee frowned, but trusting her assistant opened the letter and began reading.

In the other office, across the country, Kevin Oster also held an envelope that had been given him, he pulled out the pages and began reading.

If someone could see the two faces as they read the contents of the letters, the looks would have been identical.

At first skeptical, then curious and then finally both Renee and Kevin in their separate offices had the same "I gotcha" smile on their faces.

Both knew the story from years back when the two doctors had been facing charges of malpractice and unethical conduct. Both had expected the inevitable, but had still been disappointed when Doctor Sullivan and Doctor Harrell had been cleared of all charges thanks to their high priced lawyers.

Both Renee and Kevin in offices miles apart reached for their phones at the same time. Two calls were made by each of them.

The first was to the Portsmouth newspaper and the second was to the airlines to get the first available flight headed to Portsmouth.

Chapter 16

Natalie smiled as she turned to look at Tony. The two of them were sitting in paradise. The seats they were on weren't man made. They looked like it though. Mother Nature or some force similar had seemed to carve the seats out of a large rock. Natalie had been surprised the first time she had seen the rocks. Tony had only laughed and explained that in the other worlds anything might be found.

The two had found the place that at first was nothing more than a lean-to, when they had taken shelter here. That was when they had first stepped through the doorway and into what to Natalie looked like heaven.

Now, two months later, they had built the once lean-to into what was more like something you'd find on a beach on an island somewhere. The small place had three rooms that sat in front of the lush growth of the area. Tony had fashioned them a bathroom back in the dark green bushes. Instead of a shower they had a blue ocean to swim in and Natalie couldn't be happier.

Still she knew they couldn't stay forever. She wanted to go back and see what had become of her fellow workers and find out what had happened to the two doctors who had used devious and unprofessional means to make money and fame for themselves, despite the lives they shattered. If nothing had been done she knew it was up to her and Tony to bring the crimes out in the open.

Natalie and Tony had already made a few trips back to Portsmouth. Most late at night to twenty four hour grocery stores for supplies. Natalie knew that soon they'd have to make the trip in the daytime hours, but for now, all she wanted to do was sit back and enjoy the time with the man who had brought her here and who she loved with all her heart and soul.

P.S. Winn

As always, thanks to readers for picking up the book. I hope the story took you away from reality for a short while.

I am fascinated by parallel worlds and readers can find them in a lot of my stories. I also seem to be fascinated by hypnosis as I have that in a few stories as well. Although in my stories hypnotism is not always used to help others or used by good people, I think it is an amazing and helpful way to accomplish some wonderful things, especially health wise.
It is however interesting to look at the other side of the coin and what some people would do if they could use hypnosis. If I had the ability I'm not sure what I would do, but I have many family members and friends with chronic conditions I would love to be able to help. The only therapy I offer is the short time my stories take them away from the pains and trials of life.

I hope my stories do that.

I hoped you enjoyed the story and will look for more P.S. Winn books on Amazon and Barnes and Noble. Just type in my name, I have quite a few books to look at.

Check out the other titles from P.S. Winn

<u>Novels</u>

Foretold
Voices
Obligations
Tunnels
Capernicious
B.A. 47
Pacific Passage
Suppression
Lies in Shadows
Phases
Mystic Valley

The New Moon Killer
Healings
Superstition Canyon
Collisions
Viewings
At Hidden Lake
A Gradual Decline
Judgments
Of Jeebies and Journey
Into The Doorways
Correlations
Parallel Adventures - Into the Caves
Parallel Adventures - Secrets Revealed

Collections

Visitations
Heartfelts
Wings to Whispers
Stretched Stories
Stretched Stories 2
Tidbits and Treasure
Life Bridges

Comic books

The Golden Years
The Golden Years 2

For Children

The Alphabet Book
The Number Book
The Secret Life of Goats
No, Jimmy, No

I hope you enjoy the books as much as I enjoyed putting them on paper.

P.S. Winn